FLORID.

Author's Revised Edition
(Fourth Thousand)

𝒮𝒯𝒪𝑅𝒴 𝒪𝐹 𝒯𝐻𝐸 𝐻𝒰𝒢𝒰𝐸𝒩𝒪𝒯𝒮

A Sixteenth Century Narrative Wherein the French, Spaniards and Indians Were the Actors

F. A. Mann

HERITAGE BOOKS
2009

HERITAGE BOOKS
AN IMPRINT OF HERITAGE BOOKS, INC.

Books, CDs, and more—Worldwide

For our listing of thousands of titles see our website
at
www.HeritageBooks.com

A Facsimile Reprint
Published 2009 by
HERITAGE BOOKS, INC.
Publishing Division
100 Railroad Ave. #104
Westminster, Maryland 21157

Copyright © 1898, 1912 F. A. Mann

Index Copyright © 2002 Heritage Books, Inc.

— Publisher's Notice —
In reprints such as this, it is often not possible to remove blemishes from the original. We feel the contents of this book warrant its reissue despite these blemishes and hope you will agree and read it with pleasure.

International Standard Book Numbers
Paperbound: 978-0-7884-2173-0
Clothbound: 978-0-7884-8077-5

Dedication for New Edition

He surely can be counted a friend who steps out into the storm to welcome another to a haven of shelter and rest, saying "Peace be with you! Make this your home until God gives you another."

A stranger in a far land, compelled by Providence or Fate, whichever one may name it, when beyond the allotted span of human life, to resume a strenuous task long laid aside, the author dedicates this revised edition of The Story of The Huguenots to

DR. H. C. DIMOCK
For that indeed, he was just such a friend.

Florian A. Mann

Lompoc, California, Sept. 12th, 1911.

FLORIDA

Neither prose, however deftly written by a master of language; or poetry full of the subtlest, grandest inspiration; or the art of the painter, however well the artist hand and pencil may respond to ideal conceptions of scenic beauty; can more than approximate a presentation of Florida to the mind of one who has not wandered in its forests, stood by its sea, lake and river shores, breathed its balmy air and rejoiced in its sunshine.

On all the surface of this great globe, Florida is, unique and matchless in its peculiarities of climate, soil and topography.

In the latitude of the great African Sahara, washed by the same ocean, the climate and scenery of this peninsular region is at every point the opposite. So with its soil; its many and varied agricultural productions; its animal life, indigenous or domesticated; its general surface and configuration.

More than three centuries ago the first settlement of Europeans was made upon her shores, yet to-day an hour's walk or ride from the boundaries of any of her towns will take one into the primitive wilderness of forest and savanna, dale, hammock or cypress bay, wherein Ponce de Leon lost himself nearly four hundred years ago.

Fire swept, war swept, though the land has been again and again, yet nature ever regains her dominion and erases the traces of attempted conquest. The hordes of painted savages, the bannered armies of later days, have melted into the earth and left no lasting traces behind. The lofty pines throw down their fragrant needles in soft carpets over the paths worn by their feet. The flowers and the grasses hide their camping grounds and their graves alike from sight.

Changeless, yet ever changing and forever beautiful, Florida is still the fair temple of nature as erected at the first, for as yet the hand of man has added or marred but little.

Still, as in the prehistoric times, the tides lap her silver beaches along more than a thousand miles of shore. Her rivers flow with tranquil currents to every point of the compass untrammeled by man, yet furnishing easy channels for his commerce or weirdly beautiful ones for his pleasures. Her great, clear fountains well up from subterranean reservoirs bounteous and exhaustless as ever. Her thousand lakelets and inland seas flash back like polished silver mirrors the glorious sunshine of continuous summer days or the jewelling stars of nights equally as perfect. So too, as always since known to human beings, wild or half way civilized, the winds of heaven bring to all its parts, inland or coastland, sweetness, health and coolness.

Here no sirocco comes with burning breath to shrivel up flower and leaf, blade of corn or grass. No blizzard comes from polar zones to bind in fetters of icy death. No cyclones tear down her palms and pines, her sturdy, stately oaks and their congeners, mingling uprooted trunks and mangled limbs with wrecks of human fabrics.

Nor yet as in other lands that would rival this, does nature in a mood of anarchy and chaos, hold aloft the volcano's torch or rock and cleave the earth with earthquake horrors. Here she shows her gentlest spirit and bids love reign, in beauty, peace and comfort.

Here she woos men to come and build their homes, by stream or lake or ocean shore, with the voices of gentle waves, the aeolian harps of pine forests or the unrivaled minstrelsy of feathered songsters who surely learned their notes hard by the gates of Eden.

Vain is the attempt to idealize Florida, as master minds have other lands. She has no Aegean sea, no vale of Tempe, no Parnassus or Olympian heights; no blue tideless Mediterranean, no snow crowned Alps or Appenines. Few are her sad stories of human woes and misery, lurid with war and conflagration, brightened with sunbursts of glory and victory, blackened with the despair of ages.

Yet can she forego all these and still be as fair a land as any under the sun for this is what she is as God and nature made her.

Preliminary Historical Notes

In 1512, Juan Ponce de Leon, Spanish governor of Porto Rico, fitted out three ships at his own expense, for a voyage of discovery. He was an old soldier, brave and skillful in the art of war, but ignorant and credulous. He was lured to Florida by tales of a miraculous fountain of youth somewhere within its borders.

He sailed from Porto Rico March 13th, 1513, and on the 6th of April discovered a fair land to which, from the abundance of flowers found in its forests and the day upon which he discovered it, Easter Sunday, or as the Spaniards call it Pascua Florida, he gave the name it still bears. It is not certain at what place he first landed but on the 12th of April he landed in the vicinity where St. Augustine now stands, and taking formal possession of the country for Spain, proceeded to explore its coast. It is needless to say that he failed to find both youth and gold, and that on his second expedition a few years later his little army was broken up in warring with the natives and he himself was mortally wounded.

The expeditions of Pamphilo de Narvaez in 1528 and Ferdinand de Soto in 1539, the latter of which landed at Tampa, in the end shared the same fate; Narvaez drowning with the bulk of his followers in the Gulf of Mexico and De Soto dying on the banks of the Mississippi.

These expeditions were more marauding and plundering ones than anything else, resulting in little good except to add to geographical knowledge.

The first attempt at practical, permanent colonization, was made by Admiral Coligny of France, who sought to provide a refuge for the French Huguenots in Florida. In 1562 he sent out under Jean Ribault and Rene Laudonniere two vessels with colonists and supplies. They first sighted land near Mosquito Inlet and coasting northward discovered the mouth of the St. Johns, which they called the River of May. "He was met on its shores by many of the native men and women. These received him with gentleness and peace." They made orations to each other which neither understood except their kindly import and exchanged presents. The genial, kindly Frenchmen were greeted everywhere with "grace and gentleness by a goodly people of lively wit and fine stature."

Sometimes when the Huguenots landed first, the natives fled to their coverts but were soon coaxed back by them and "persuaded finally to confidence." The native Floridians "brought forward gifts of maize, palm baskets of fruit and flowers and dressed skins of bear and deer."

Laudonniere speaks of the "odorous flowers, the fish swarming in the streams, the game in the forests, the gardens and villages of pleasant, peaceable people."

However, this expedition made no attempt at colonization within the present limits of Florida. This was not done until 1564, when a settlement was established on the St. Johns near its mouth and left in charge of Laudonniere. The bloodly tale of its destruction by Melendez in 1565 is one of the many black pages of Spanish history.

PART I.

Story of the Huguenots.
THE HISTORY OF IT.

CHAPTER I.
FOUNDING OF LA CAROLINE.

The first expedition of Ribault and Laudonniere in 1562 established no colony within the limits of Florida. It however attempted a settlement at Port Royal in South Carolina which was abandoned in 1563, the colonists building a rude brigantine in which they attempted to return to France. They nearly perished by famine but were picked up by an English vessel and taken home.

In 1564, through the influence of the great Admiral of France, Coligny, a second expedition was fitted out of three ships and the new armament was assigned to the command of Laudonniere, a man of intelligence, a good seaman rather than a soldier. He found it easy enough not only to procure sailors for his ships but settlers for the proposed colony.

He and those with him on the former expedition were able to testify truly to the "wonderful beauty of the country, the sweetness of the climate, the richness and variety of its fruits and flowers, the game in its forests, the multitudes of fine fish in its waters." Many still believed in De Leon's fountain of youth and in the dreams of rich cities and mines of gold and silver hidden somewhere in its boundaries, that animated De Soto.

It did not matter that heretofore death had kept the

portals of the country. They were men who had defied him in the many battle fields of the civil wars which had raged in France for years. Not only did many soldiers volunteer, but workers and artisans in abundance.

The passion for adventure, exploration and conquest had been raised to the highest pitch in the military class by the exploits of Cortez, Pizarro, Balboa and those of De Leon and De Soto, unfortunate as they were; while to the oppressed artisans and peasantry of Europe the new fertile lands, unbounded in extent and virgin, with the promise of a freedom not possible at home had great attraction. In fact far more volunteers presented themselves than could be accommodated and on the 22nd of April, 1564, the expedition sailed from France in high hopes and expectations.

A voyage of two months brought them to the shores of Florida, June 25th, near the same latitude as on the former expedition. The delight of the voyagers may be imagined when, on entering the River May, the San Mateo of the Spaniards, the St. Johns of the present day, they found themselves warmly welcomed by the natives, especially those who were recognized as former visitors with Ribault. It was at a period of the year for seeing the country in its greatest loveliness. The noble river, capacious enough for all the French navy to anchor in, the beautiful wooded shores lined with silvery beaches, the genial temperature combined with the kindly welcome given, raised their spirits to the highest pitch.

When they landed, they were conducted by a large concourse of natives, with great ceremonials, to the spot where Ribault had set up a stone column carved with the arms of France "upon a little sandy knappe, not far from the mouth of said river." With pleased surprise, Laudonniere found the pillar encircled and covered with wreaths of flowers and around its base were set little baskets of maize, beans and other products brought in great abundance as gifts to their visitors.

"The Indians kissed the column which they had consecrated in memory of former friendship and made the French do likewise." Their Chief presented Laudonniere with a "wedge of silver," a gift that led the Frenchmen to dream of great riches to be found somewhere in the land. Naturally they associated gold with silver and were assured that both were to be found amongst their enemies, the boundaries of whose territory came to the River May and extended far northward to a high mountain region.

It is evident from the narrative that the natives who were first met by the Frenchmen were the original inhabitants of the land; that they were a gentler race than those living to the northward and that the latter in time being more warlike eventually drove them southward, finally either exterminating them or absorbing the broken fragments into their own body.

Laudonniere sailed up the river and was everywhere received with kindness. They mutually called each other "friends and brothers." He then coasted northward almost to Port Royal or Fort Charles.

Laudonniere returned with his vessels from this cruise to the River May the latter part of June, 1564, having abandoned the idea of re-establishing the settlement at Fort Charles, of the fate of which the Indians had informed him, with the determination to found his Huguenot colony in the neighborhood of the beautiful river with which he had become acquainted on the previous voyage.

The reasons for this preference are given in his own language, abbreviating and modernizing somewhat:

"If we passed farther to the north to seek out Port Royal it would be neither profitable nor convenient, although that haven is one of the fairest of the West Indies. In this case the question is not so much the beauty of the place as of the things necessary to sustain life. For our inhabitation it is much more needful for us to plant in places plentiful of victual than goodly havens, fair, deep and pleasant to the view. In consideration whereof I am of opinion, if it seems good to the company, to seat ourselves about the River of May, seeing that in our first voyage we found the same only to abound in maize and other corn." The wedge of silver presented to him on his former visit and a few ornaments of gold doubtless were the conclusive suggestions.

Anchoring at the mouth of the river, which, from the scanty description left in the old chronicles, although contended by some to be the St. Mary's conforms more to the St. Johns, Laudonniere took his pinnace and a number of the proposed colonists and sailed into it in search of a place for settlement. The result was the selection of a bluff on the south side of the river, evidently not far from its mouth, covered with a thick and high wood and close to what he calls "a great vale. In form flat, wherein were the finest meadows of the world and grass to feed cattle, with brooks of fresh water and high woods which made the vale delectable to the eyes." This he called the vale of Laudonniere.

On this bluff at the break of day on the 30th of June, 1564, the trumpets were sounded and the Huguenots were called to prayer, and so, long prior to the landing of the Pilgrim Fathers at Plymouth was celebrated the Protestant worship within the present limits of Florida.

After this they applied themselves diligently to the erection of a fortress, triangular in shape, the landward side built of fagots, sand and turf, with a ditch, and the river side a palisade of planks or heavy timbers. Within it were built barracks, a house for the commandant, an arsenal, presumably of logs from the adjacent forests and thatched with palmetto leaves.

In the neighborhood of the fort there were rich spots which afforded facilities for gardening, but so eager was Laudonniere to find gold and silver—an eagerness that was shared by all the company—that leaving only a few to guard the fort he commenced the exploration of the country, leading or sending out expeditions in various directions in search of the precious metals, some of which covered a large portion of Florida, Georgia and even South Carolina. If the narrative is to be credited, plates of gold and silver were secured from the native tribes to the northward in sufficient quantities to keep the colonists employed in this pursuit to the neglect of every other. For many months he and his lieutenants, Ottigny, D'Erlach, LeGenre and Captain Vasseur, pushed their gold and silver seeking expeditions, frequently involving conflicts with the Indians, more especially with the warlike confederacy, whose territories stretched from the Appalachian mountains southward to the borders of the River May, whom they called *Thimogoans.

According to the tales of River May Indians the Thimogoan warriors covered their breasts and foreheads with plates of gold and silver, and it is probable that inhabitating a country in which both metals have since been found, there was some foundation for these statements which were, however, much exaggerated. It is said that Chevalier D'Erlach returned from one of the most successful of these expeditions with no inconsiderable spoils of gold, silver, painted skins and other Indian commodities.

These expeditions, however, by no means compensated in their results for the evils the Huguenots were bringing on themselves in neglecting their settlement at La Caroline, the cultivation of the natural resources of the country, and were preparing the way for the terrible calamity which fell upon it.

(*Query—Was this not the name from which Tomoka is derived, for in the wars which were prosecuted after this date these northern Indians succeeded in driving still farther southward the weaker and more peaceable coast tribe, until they occupied the neighborhood of the Tomoka and were long known by that name, to the time when they too were finally driven out by the Spaniards and English and plantations established where once were their populous villages.)

CHAPTER II.
FAMINE COMES—BATTLE WITH THE INDIANS.

During many months but little improvement was made by the colonists of La Caroline in the way of utilizing the fertility of the soil in the production of food or even in strengthening the defences. As the winter passed away in constant expeditions after precious metals their stores rapidly decreased. They expected a renewal of supplies and an increase to their numbers through the arrival of Ribault from France with a fleet of vessels which, through Admiral Coligny's aid he was to fit out. But they watched long in vain. The expedition was delayed by troubles in France and in the meantime a famine came upon the Huguenots, greatly as a result of their own recklessness.

In May, Laudonniere himself describes their straits as very desperate:

"We were constrained to eat roots, which the most part of our men pounded in the mortars which I had brought with me to beat gunpowder in, and the grain which came from other places. Some took the wood of esquine (probably cabbage palmetto) beat it and made meal thereof which they boiled and ate. Others went with their arquebuses to kill fowl," and so on with a pathetic description of the weakness and sickness brought on by famine, finishing with reciting how the colonists not being able to work "did nothing but goe one after another, as centinals, unto the cliffe of a hill very near unto the fort, to see if they might discover any French ship."

Finally their hopes deferred making them heart sick they pressed their commander to attempt the building of a vessel which, with the small one they had, would enable them to sail back to France.

There were good shipwrights among them and to these Laudonniere deputed the task of building the new vessel while he undertook to scour the coast for provisions of any kind that might be found, but the expeditions which had traversed the neighboring territory had weakened the friendship and confidence of the natives with whom also at that time of the year there was no superfluous stock of provisions left.

Laudonniere returned unsuccessful from a coastwise voyage of forty to fifty leagues and the colonists, now desperate with hunger, riotously insisted that the only way to extort food from the savages was to seize upon the person of one of their kings and secure it as ransom. To this at first their commander would not consent. He proposed a trial of the friendship of the natives and sent messages to open up traffic for food with the surrounding tribes. But the Indians knew the urgency of the case and proposed to turn it to account. They came to the garrison with small amounts of food for which they asked enormous prices. When Laudonniere remonstrated, they tauntingly answered:

"If thou make such great account of thy merchandise, let it stay thy hunger. Eat it and we will eat our grain."

In the end and goaded beyond endurance Laudonniere resolved on doing as his people counseled.

Story of the Huguenots

Two of his barks and a body of fifty men were chosen for an expedition to the capital town of the chief, who ruled a large contiguous territory. This was forty or fifty leagues up the river and six or more leagues inland. One of his officers, D'Erlach, had been there before and knew the way.

They made the voyage successfully to the point of debarkation; left a guard in their vessels and marching inland succeeded in taking the Indian village by surprise. They, however, made no hostile demonstration on entering the village, Laudonniere still hoping to obtain peacefully what he needed, and so parleyed with the chief. But while the chief did not hesitate to supply the immediate wants of the Frenchmen, he declined to furnish any considerable amount of provisions. In fact he argued that they were in a great measure responsible themselves for their destitute condition. He said: "Hath the Great Spirit commanded that the red man shall gather food in the proper season that the white man may sleep like the drowsy deer in the palmetto thicket?"

It was true, but it was also true that their wants admitted of no denial; and after a vain attempt to barter for food Laudonniere gave the signal to seize the chief which was promptly done.

Then a war conch was sounded to rally the Indian warriors which was answered by D'Erlach's bugler calling in the stragglers scattered through the village in quest of food and the retreat to the riverside began.

The capture of the Chief Olata Utina was so unexpected and the retreat to the river so rapidly and skillfully executed that no chance was given the Indians to rally in sufficient force to prevent it.

It was, however, Laudonniere's intent to treat with them for food and not to engage in any hostile contest if it could be avoided, and so he opened a parley with the savages assembled on the banks of the river, proposing to release the chief upon their delivering a certain quantity of maize, beans, dried venison, etc. But the Indians were suspicious, believing the Frenchmen, after obtaining what they desired would not release him; and after fruitless attempts to obtain provisions with but a small quantity that had been obtained in the village, the expedition returned to La Caroline, taking also the chief, who was treated kindly but kept in confinement, which was very irksome to him.

By dint of plundering the villages of some Indian tribes that had been guilty of unfriendly and hostile acts, fishing and hunting, the people of La Caroline managed to maintain life in a meagre fashion. Finally the old chief proposed that they take him back to his people and permit him to use his influence with them, telling his captors the maize was then about ripe and promising to use his best efforts in behalf of the Frenchmen. So the two little barks again sailed up the river.

Long before they came to anchor at the landing, Olata Utina's people gathered in great numbers, hardly knowing what to expect. Negotiations were opened by Laudonniere, who informed them that he was willing to release their chief to them for a quantity of provisions which to the Frenchmen seemed small, but to the Indians was a heavy ransom. It would sweep their little fields and granaries bare, even taking the very seed necessary for future harvests. Their love for their chief was not small, but it was of the last importance to free him without subjecting themselves to risk of famine. So they exercised all their arts of stratagem and diplomacy to secure that end without paying too dearly. They brought considerable supplies of food which they gave to the Frenchmen, but no definite end was reached for several days during which many hundreds of warriors gathered in the vicinity. But Laudonniere was vigilant and finding that attempts to rescue the chief or to capture Laudonniere himself so that they might exchange chief for chief, could not be made successful, an agreement was finally entered into by which Olata Utina was to be freed, two chiefs agreeing to become hostages for the delivery of the ransom, which the Indians were to gather in from all the tribal villages within a certain time.

The chronicle gives a brief description of the scene at the restoration of the chief to his people: "The two warrior hostages came on board the bark and as they approached their chief broke their bows and arrows in token of surrender. Then as they beheld his bonds, they knelt at his feet, lifted up his chains and kissed them, nor did they show any repugnance to assuming the fetters as they were loosened from Olata Utina, looking upon him with delight as he was being freed."

The chief arose from his place and shook himself like a lion rousing from sleep. Never was head held more erect or form more stately. He waved his hand to the shore where his people were gathered. The signal was evidently understood for one of his sons came out in a canoe bringing a mantle of fringed and gorgeously dyed grass cloth, his macana or war club, and a mighty bow with arrows five feet long.

Throwing the mantle over his shoulders, he took the bow and, before he left the vessel fitted an arrow to it, letting it fly out of sight into the air as a signal that he was once more free. A cloud of arrows from the shore followed that of their sovereign and wild shouts echoed far across the broad river.

The liberated chief had agreed to the terms of the Frenchmen, but stipulated that he should have a certain number of days in which to gather the supplies. Laudonniere left his lieutenants with a strong detachment of soldiers, one of the barks and the two hostages to await the issue while he returned to La Caroline.

The upshot of the whole business was that after two or three days of waiting, word was sent to them that they must bring their hostages to the village and there receive the ransom. Olata had found it impossible to compel his people to promptly comply with the stipulations. They absolutely refused to bring any supplies down to the river. He, however, was honorably disposed to keep his word and thought their presence in the capital town would have the effect to make the people act more promptly.

So they marched on the town, keeping their arquebuses loaded with the matches burning ready to repel any attack that might be made upon them. They reached the village in safety although the woods swarmed with warriors who were apparently only kept at bay by fear of the deadly fire arms and the vigilance of the Frenchmen.

The dwelling house and council chamber of Olata Utina was on an "artificial eminence," probably a mound such as are still to be found in all parts of Florida. Here they found assembled all the chiefs of the nation except their former prisoner. To a certain extent his authority to treat with the Frenchmen was usurped by these chiefs, who were evidently determined to deal with the invaders themselves, using craft and dissimulation to throw them off their guard and then seize the first opportunity to overpower them. But D'Erlach and Ottigny were experienced in savage habits and were not to be deceived by the apparently friendly reception given them.

The Indians pointed to the sacks of meal and beans piled up on the council floor and showed the Frenchmen others being newly brought in. Then commenced a palaver designed to allay suspicions, but which had the contrary effect. At nightfall a private conference was held with Olata Utina. He informed them that his anxiety to comply with his engagements had impaired his authority; that the chief warriors had resolved to destroy the pale faces as invaders, consumers of their substance and destroyers of their peace. He advised them to retreat to their vessel and La Caroline with all haste, for from all quarters were gathering the warriors and there were only pretences made to carry out the treaty.

The despondency of the chief was without hypocrisy. His warnings were sincere. But the necessity of securing all the supplies they could prompted the Frenchmen to tarry the full period of four days and in the meantime they urged on the accumulation.

Finally, seeing that no more was being brought in they released their hostages and on the morning of July 27th prepared for the retreat to their bark. Each soldier was required to load himself with as much provisions as he could carry, the chiefs having flatly refused to furnish any carriers and for the last time in this region the French bugles blew the signal of marching.

BATTLE OF TAGASETA.

Not far did they go, however, before the battle they anticipated began. The woods swarmed with warriors armed with stone hatchets, war clubs and bows. But they had learned a wholesome respect for the arquebuses or matchlocks of the French and so their volleys of arrows were delivered at too great a distance to do much damage. However, as the road lay through hammock belts where the timber was thick it was soon found necessary to send out flanking parties to drive the Indians from their coverts and to disencumber themselves of their burdens of provisions so that they could more effectively handle their weapons. Seeing their enemies halt for this purpose, and mistaking it for a sign of fear, the Indians advanced closer, filling the woods with their yells, and delivered a volley of arrows that fell among the little squadron. Their steel caps and leather doublets, however, proved excellent defences against the flint and bone headed shafts and D'Erlach said to his men: "Do not answere them yet, but stoop ye every man and break as many arrows as ye can. Blow your matches as ye do so and when they come close let the first rank deliver fire." He had observed that the enemy gathered up the arrows as they passed and used them again.

The command was obeyed with coolness by the arquebusiers and the result was when the savages made a concerted rush they were met with a volley of bullets which killed many and momentarily scattered the rest. New bands of savages, however, constantly appeared to harass the retreat and the whole day long the battle waged. The Frenchmen were compelled to economize their ammunition and forebore to shoot except when it was absolutely necessary. But the courage of the red men increased as the battle spirit warmed up and they bravely contested every foot of the way, even though their weapons and military skill were deficient. Great havoc was made among them, but never men fought more bravely than they did. It is written of them, in Laudonniere's quaint record, "All the while they had their eye and foot so quick and redie, that as soon as ever they saw the harquebuse raised to the cheek, so soon were they on the ground, eftsoone to answere with their bowes and to flie away when we were about to take them."

The conflict ceased at nightfall when weary and exhausted the Frenchmen, of whom twenty-four were killed and wounded, chiefly the latter, reached their boats. The Floridians had shown themselves warriors of spirit and capacity. They had driven out the invaders, recovered the booty, rescued the hostages and if they had lost seriously so had their enemies. Reading the chronicle one is reminded that for more than two centuries they with the same indomitable spirit kept Spain and England at bay and finally only yielded after a heroic struggle, to soldiers forest born, like themselves, the best riflemen of the south led by Jackson, Taylor and Harney.

CHAPTER III.
ARRIVAL OF SIR JOHN HAWKINS AND RETURN OF RIBAULT.

After all the toil and sacrifice of several brave men, it was found to be impossible to supply the colonists of La Caroline sufficiently to put them in good condition or good heart. Indeed the home sickness under which they labored had reached such a height as to admit of no appeal or argument. Cruel as France had been to the Huguenots, she was yet France and the memory of her green vales and vine clad hills was not to be replaced by the glorious beauty, even in its savagery, of the shores of the River May.

Their discontents grew into a passionate longing for return and when it was found that the building of the vessel which had been commenced for that purpose would be delayed by the death in battle of two of the carpenters, they mutinously set upon Jean De Hais, the master carpenter, because he had declared it would be impossible to complete it by the specified time and it was with difficulty he was saved from the mob.

There was still left of the original vessels which brought them an old brigantine and Laudonniere finding he was compelled to give up the original design of building a new vessel addressed all of his energies to its repair. Determined to leave nothing behind when they were ready to depart his men tore down the houses which had been erected outside of the fort to make coal for the forge and also the palisades leading from the fort to the river, thus greatly weakening their defences, in spite of their governor's objections.

Laudonniere was indeed very loath to give up the colony he had done so much to establish. It distressed him greatly that the promise of succor from France expected with the return of Ribault was delayed so long.

On the afternoon of the third of August, Laudonniere took a walk as was his daily custom, to the top of a little eminence, near the fort, which offered a prospect of the sea. Looking forth to the eastward over the vast watery waste, he was greatly excited to see the sails of four approaching vessels. The joy of the garrison was great for they naturally supposed Ribault was coming. Laudonniere writes quaintly: "Soe great was their gladness at this that one would have believed them to be out of their wittes, to see them laugh and leap."

But the ships, instead of sailing boldly in as Ribault should have done, approached cautiously. Finally they cast anchor and sent out a boat toward the shore. A prudent fear of the Spaniards prompted Laudonniere to call the garrison to arms and send a detachment to meet the visitors at the river side. They hailed in French and in the same language came the reply, stating that the ships were those of the famous Admiral Hawkins on an exploring expedition. With him was Martin Atinas of Dieppe, one of the former colonists of deserted Fort Charles, picked up at sea and carried to Europe, who had piloted the squadron.

The object of the British Admiral was pacific, nor was it long before his generous and noble conduct won the hearts of the Huguenots. He saw their distressful plight and gave them liberal supplies of wine and provisions. With even greater liberality and a wise policy, seeing their discontent, he offered to transport the whole colony to France. But Laudonniere was still hoping for the return of Ribault and a surer foundation for the colony, so declined the proposition which had been made to him only as a commanding officer. However, to make sure of the means to return if pressed to it, he bargained with Hawkins for one of his vessels. The consideration given by Laudonniere was a portion of the military furniture of the fort, particularly described as "Two bastards, two mynions, one thousand iron balls and one thousand pounds of powder, etc."

Moved with pity for the wretched condition of the Frenchmen, the generous Englishman offered supplies for which he accepted Laudonniere's bills, which the letter's subsequent misfortunes never permitted him to cancel. These supplies included "twenty barrels of meal, six pipes of beanes, one hogshead of salt and a hundred (cwt.) of waxe to make candles. Moreover, forasmuch as he saw my souldiers goe barefoote he offered me besides fifty paires of shoes which I accepted. He did more than this: he bestowed upon myself a great jar of oil, a jar of vinegar, a barrel of olives, a great quantity of rice and a barrel of white biscuits. Besides he gave divers presents to the principal officers of my company according to their quality; so that I may say we received as many courtesies of the General as was possible to expect of any man."

This visit of Hawkins is the brightest episode in the history of the ill fated colony. Doubtless had it been a little later or had he tarried longer the cruel Spanish wolf never would have bathed his jaws in Hugenuot gore and certainly with amity between the English and French Florida might have been a prosperous country long years ago and have been spared generations of tyranny and degradation such as curse all lands overshadowed by the flag of Spain. But it was not to be. The folly of men, then as now, was thrown athwart the wisdom of God and for a time turned this Eden of the new world into a hell of murder and rapine.

Sir John Hawkins, whose arrival at La Caroline and the noble manner in which he treated the Huguenots has thus been described, left on record many particulars interesting in themselves and also as showing the primary causes of the colony's fatal weakness. At the close of the war mentioned as resulting from the foraging expedition to the Indian villages, he relates that Laudonniere had not forty soldiers left unhurt. After detailing the supplies accorded to the colonists from his stores he adds: "Notwithstanding the great want the Frenchmen had, the ground doth yield victuals sufficient, if they had taken the pains to get the same; but they being soldiers desired to live by the sweat of other men's brows." Here speaks the jealous scorn of the sailor. "The ground yieldeth naturally great store of grapes, for in the time the Frenchmen were there they made twenty hogsheads of wine, also," says Hawkins, "the land yieldeth roots passing good, deere marvelous store, with divers other beasts and fruits serviceable to man. These be things wherewith a man may live having corn or maize wherewith to make bread, and this maize was the greatest lack they had because they had no laborers to sow the same. Had they done so," he continues, "they having victuals of their own, whereby they neither spoil nor rob the inhabitants, may live not only quietly with them who naturally are more desirous of peace than warre, but also shall have abundance of victuals proffered them for nothing," etc.

The testimony of the Admiral is conclusive as to the originally gentle and peaceful character of the oboriginal Floridians. He speaks of the country as abounding in natural resources, equal to those of any region in the world.

The account which Hawkins gives of the abundance of fish in the neighborhood is no exaggeration. It adds to the surprise of the reader at the wretched indolence or incapacity of the colonists, who, with this resource at "their doores, depended for their supply upon the Indians." He left the Huguenots on the 28th of August, 1565, making preparations to follow him. The biscuit was made, the goods and chattels were taken on board and most of the water;—nothing delayed their sailing but head winds. Laudonniere was prepared to depart when the voyage was arrested by the appearance of Ribault with the long expected supplies from France.

The approach of Ribault's vessels was exceedingly cautious; so much so that the heavier guns of the fort still left mounted were turned to bear upon them when up went the Fleur-de-Lis of France.

The relief to Laudonniere was great, for he feared they might be Spaniards, and in the present weak condition of the fort, defence was hopeless. The reasons for Ribault's action arose from certain false reports which had reached France, of the conduct of Laudonniere, letters sent secretly by malcontents when Ribault had returned to France, and fabricated reports, accusing him of preparing to shake off the sovereignty of the mother country and designing to set himself up as the sovereign lord of Florida. Poor Laudonniere, living on snakes, crude berries and bitter roots, mocked by savages on one hand, flouted by rebels defying his authority, the target for the curses of the discontented and home sick, surely was in no mood to affect royalty on the banks of the River May.

He was vain and ostentatious, perhaps; he had his faults and absurdities like other men, but he was genial hearted and brave. He had been too bitterly schooled by his adversities to dream of such idle affectations or desires. Yet, of all this the King of France nor Admiral Coligny, the projector of the colony, could know anything. Composed of Huguenots only, a people of whose fidelity the former might reasonably doubt, the Catholic King might be readily supposed to give ear to the charges, false as they were. However, Coligny, kept his promise and sent Ribault's seven vessels with a military force corresponding.

To the great relief of Ribault his old comrade received him with submission and soon succeeded in convincing him that he had been greatly slandered; that he was innocent of any assumption of royalty or of unauthorized state of any kind; that however unfortunate he might have been, he was not guilty of the follies, presumption and cruelty which constituted the several points in the indictment against him.

Ribault strove to persuade him to remain in the colony and to leave his justification to himself; but this Laudonniere declined to do, resolving to return to France, a resolution which we shall see hereafter was only delayed too long, to the further increase of the misfortunes of our captain.

Shortly after the arrival of Jean Ribault, Laudonniere fell sick with fever, and the former assumed command. Crowds of friendly Indians came to the fort, curious as to the new arrivals. They soon recognized Ribault as the chief who had raised the stone pillar at the mouth of the river. The recognition was easy by reason of the massy beard he wore. They welcomed him with the greatest cordiality and a number of the neighboring chiefs recalled the ties of former friendship with mystic ceremonies and made fresh pledges of amity. They brought to him several pieces of what in their language they called "sierra pira" or "yellow metal" which, upon being tested by the refiners, proved to be "perfect gold."

They offered to conduct Ribault to the mountains of Apalachia where it was to be found, they reported, in abundance. He was contemplating a visit to the mountains when events of the greatest importance, superseding the hopes of gain, obliged the colonists to contend for their lives. The Spaniards, of whom they had been long apprehensive, appeared upon the coast.

CHAPTER IV.
PEDRO MELENDEZ DE AVILA APPEARS.

Spain and France at this time were by treaty at peace with each other, but Spain claimed Florida by right of discovery and her jealousy had been roused by the reported attempted founding of the French colonies. Philip the Second, a cold blooded, malignant and jealous despot, freed by amnesty from the cares of war at home was now at liberty to push his conquests abroad. His great plea was his desire to spread the Catholic faith, but in reality he was moved only by a cruel and insatiable ambition and was in religion a fanatical hypocrite and bigot.

Pedro Melendez de Avila, an officer who had previously distinguished himself in other expeditions to the new world, sought and obtained the appointment of Adelantado with the hereditary government of all the Floridas, then comprising as claimed, an immense territory stretching northward to the Carolinas and along the gulf coast to the Mississippi. Under the stimulus of the news that the French were attempting to take possession of a portion of this territory, Philip increased the fleet of the expedition to twenty vessels and its force to three thousand men. It became a crusade and the eager impetus of ambition was set on fire by the usual argument of a holy war. To extirpate heresy was in accordance with the cruel bigotry of both Charles of France and Philip.

It is said that Charles, in the same spirit which afterwards prompted the horrible massacre of St. Bartholomew, had secretly surrendered the colony of Coligny to the remorseless, conscienceless monarch of Spain. Coligny well knew how little dependence could be placed upon his king in all matters pertaining to the Huguenots and as Ribault was about to depart from France on his last voyage wrote a hasty postscript to his letter of instructions as follows: "As I was closing this letter I received certain advices that Don Pedro Melendez departeth from Spain to go to the coast of New France (Florida); see that you suffer him not to encroach upon you, no more than you will suffer yourself to encroach upon him."

On the voyage out the fleet of Melendez was scattered by tempests, many vessels being lost, until on his arrival at Porto Rico he could muster but seven or eight ships. The fleet of Ribault consisted of seven vessels, the three smallest of which ascended the river to the fort. The four larger, which were men-of-war, remained in the open roadstead at the mouth of the river. Ribault, before he left the roadstead, charged his subalterns to be on guard against any vessels that might arrive, especially Spanish.

It was well he did so for one September day they descried approaching the River May six large vessels. In the absence of Ribault the squadron was inferior in force to that of Melendez. It was evening when they stood in and too late for effective action. They lowered sail, cast anchor and forbore all offensive operations; there was even communication by boat under flag of truce between the squadrons. The Ave Maria echoed musically from the one squadron in the language of Spain, the evening songs of the French from the other. The night zephyrs blew soft and fragrant from the forest lined shores. All seemed peaceful and secure. But on every vessel were alert and wakeful sentinels gazing with keen eyes through the starlight to detect the first warlike movement. It was the summer night before the storm.

In the parley that took place in the evening between the two squadrons, the Spaniards inquired by name after the chief captains and leaders of the French, betraying an intimate knowledge of facts which had been kept as secret as possible by the originators of the expedition. This was sufficient in itself to arouse the suspicions of the latter and that night the French captains held a consultation together. They decided that they were in danger of assault and prepared themselves accordingly. The men were notified to be in readiness to take their stations at a moment's notice. Arms were overhauled and in readiness; sheets and halliards made ready for hoisting sail, for, being inferior in strength but faster sailors than their foes, it was decided at the first hostile movement to cut their cables, spread their sails and make for the open sea. The Spanish vessels occupied such a position as to make any attempt to move up to Fort Caroline dangerous.

Before daylight the creaking of windlasses notified the French that the Spanish vessels were heaving home their anchors, and without delaying to do the same, by dawn their own sails were hoisted and cutting their cables they stood out to sea just as the Spanish squadron headed for them.

The six Spanish vessels pitted against the four French ones, opened fire upon them, but the range of cannon in those days was not so great as now and their shot fell short. The French wasted no shot upon their pursuers and paid more attention to showing their enemies a clean pair of heels.

The chase continued the most of the day. Finding pursuit useless the Spanish tacked towards evening and stood in for the entrance of the Selooe, called by the French the River of Dolphins, but now known as the Matanzas River and St. Augustine Inlet.

The test having shown that they were the speedier, the French vessels came about and saucily followed them to make what discoveries they could. Coming as close as they dared they found "The Trinity," the seventh and largest of the Spanish vessels, anchored off the bar. Three of their late pursuers remained just inside while the other three, regarding the rest as more than a match for the French, sailed to the landing where an encampment had already been made. Having noted these things the French returned to the River May and reported to Ribault.

In corroboration of these facts a neighboring friendly chief had sent information to Ribault, that the Spaniards had gone ashore in great numbers at Selooe, or as Melendez christened it, St. Augustine, distant across the land but eight or ten leagues from La Caroline; that they had dispossessed the natives of their houses and were busy in entrenching a regular encampment for which purpose he had disembarked his superfluous men and remained with the great ship called The Trinity, before sending the rest in search of the French.

Ribault did not have the slightest doubt as to the intention of Melendez to attack La Caroline from this point as soon as possible. Brave as a lion he resolved to take the initiative. He needed no stronger justification than the pursuit and firing on his vessels by the Spanish fleet. The royal banner of France had been hostilely assailed although the two nations were nominally at peace with each other.

CHAPTER V.
RIBAULT'S ATTACK ON ST. AUGUSTINE—THE STORM.

Ribault called a council with all his officers in Laudonniere's chamber at La Caroline, that captain still being ill with fever. There he arrayed the arguments in favor of attacking the Spaniards at St. Augustine before they could complete their defensive arrangements. His plan was to fall upon them with all his forces by sea, boldly attacking The Trinity at anchor when the rest were in no condition to support her, and the troops of the Adelantado were partly on shore and partly on the other vessels busily engaged in the removal of material for the settlement.

Laudonniere, however, objected to Ribault's plan. La Caroline was in almost a defenceless condition; it was the season of the year as he had found by experience when sudden storms might be expected. Some of the other captains sided with him but Ribault, old sailor and gallant soldier, was eager for the fray. He did not give Laudonniere the credit he deserved for skill and courage.

He took his own course and ordered all of his own men on board his seven vessels. But not satisfied with this he took also from the fort nearly all the able bodied men and on the eighth of September parted with Laudonniere for the last time.

Scarcely had he crossed the roadstead when his vessels met squally weather, the precursor of the violent storm which followed. Ribault held on, however, to the

Story of the Huguenots

southward and in a few hours his squadron was off St. Augustine Inlet.

Had he been well acquainted with the channel and sailed boldly in, scarcely anything could have prevented a complete victory over the Spaniards. The two heavier vessels, relieved of their armament and troops, which had been transferred to the land, had been dispatched to Hispaniola. The remaining five vessels were unequal in strength to Ribault's.

Three of the latter's lighter vessels were sent in to take soundings and lead the way while the others worked after them slowly. The hours lost in this decided the fate of the Huguenots. Had they passed straight in upon their foes, the latter could have made no effective defence.

Two only of Melendez' vessels, on board one of which the Adelantado himself embarked, were ready for battle when the French were sighted. Their armament was inferior, but Melendez hoped to delay the entrance of Ribault until all the forces at his command could be rallied.

Melendez was as brave as Ribault. Both were stimulated by a fierce hatred on the score of religion. The Huguenot hated the Spaniards as Catholics, and they hated him and his followers as heretics. Each in his own estimation would be doing God service by ridding the world of the other.

Melendez exhorted his men, who were fearful of the odds against them, to be brave and prophesied a miracle would occur to deliver them from their enemies.

In the very moment when the hands of Ribault were stretched out to grasp the prize of victory which should annihilate Spanish power in Florida, the squalls suddenly changed to a north-east gale that broke upon the French squadron with the roar of a thousand lions.

The waves arose and mad foam capped billows broke clear across the channel. With a groan of rage and disappointment, Ribault was compelled to abandon the assualt and turn his attention to the safety of his vessels. Like the froth of the waves they flew southward before the mighty power of the hurricane, speeding along the white sand belted coast with no harbor of refuge for them.

Whatever their faults, their virtues, their heroism, the aroused forces of nature cared naught for them, seeming only desirous to doom them to pitiless destruction.

Darkness and storm engulfed them and through it all they could only see the phosphorescent glare of the breakers upon the shore and hear naught but their thunder.

The hollow concave of the heavens was filled with spray and darkness, save when the lightning flashes threw a ghastly glare upon the tumultuous waters.

In the meantime the Spaniards from the depths of their previous abandonment to despair, were exalted to the highest pitch of enthusiasm and rejoicing. Melendez had promised that God should work a miracle to save them. He shrewdly turned the storm to advantage in stimulating the faith and devotion of his people.

"See," said he, "what wonders God has done for you this day. Call you this the cause of our king only? It is the cause of the King of Kings! We are few, we are feeble, in a wilderness swarming with savages, but He will overcome them for us as He has already driven to destruction those heretics, the spawn of Satan! The cause in which we strive is holy. The God of storms and battles has ranged himself upon our side."

Cries of exultation answered him. A thousand voices renewed their vows of fidelity and swore to follow where he should lead. He commanded a solemn mass should be celebrated in the morning and that all the army should be present.

He knew it would be long, if ever, before the French vessels returned and already planned the utter destruction of La Caroline before succor should come.

Don Pedro Melendez de Avila was a man of rare energy, extraordinary foresight and indomitable will. His religious fanaticism, if real, gave the sanction of religion to his relentless cruelty, a savage trait of the Spanish character then as now. But the history of the whole matter shows that, after all, it was not so much the difference of creeds that made Melendez resolute for the utter destruction of the heretics of La Carolina but because he believed it absolutely essential for the continued existence of the Spanish colony that the French should be destroyed. He but played upon the ignorant fanaticism of his followers to stimulate them to work to that end with all their energies.

This design, however, the continued succession of stormy weather and the unsettled condition of affairs in his new colony of St. Augustine, compelled him to postpone for some days while he was busily engaged in erecting fortifications and dwellings for his people, during which the temporary enthusiasm created by the late apparently providential deliverance from their enemies died away in a great measure.

The mass of the Spanish colonists were not veteran soldiers, for to that class which in that marvelous age of Spanish conquest and glory abounded in Spain, the rich fields of Mexico, Central and South America offered far greater inducements, but were new recruits, or peasantry undisciplined and inexperienced in such hardships as they were now compelled to endure. There was soon consequently much murmuring and discontent.

But if the Spaniards at St. Augustine felt their hardships so greatly and their state was disheartening, much more so was the condition of affairs at La Caroline. Weakened by the departure of Ribault, of whose fate they could only conjecture; knowing only through the agency of Indian friends that the squadron had failed to accomplish its purpose and had been driven off by the gale, which had been followed by heavy rains and violent winds, the Huguenots at La Caroline were in a more deplorable state than ever. The supplies brought out by Ribault for them had been chiefly appropriated for the use of the fleet. A survey made immediately after his departure led to the stinting of the daily allowance for the garrison reduced as it was. Laudonniere was still sick; the men were spiritless, hopeless and consequently the work of repairing the defences went on but slowly, and even its watch was maintained with doubtful vigilance. Themselves much averse to exposure, they thought the Spaniards would not undertake any attempt upon the fort during the equinoctial storms, when marching through the rains and wading morasses would be likely to bring upon them malarial fevers and other sickness, and were neglectful of their duties. Languid with the fever of half healed wounds, or full of malarial poison, enfeebled with scant food, even the bravest veterans among them had lost heart and had sunk into a state of apathy from which it was impossible to arouse them.

Not even Laudonniere could blame them, although he had reason to believe that at some unexpected moment his cruel and wily enemy would aim his heaviest blows upon their heads.

Leaving the unfortunate Huguenots of La Carolina, let us turn again to the Spaniards at St. Augustine.

The energy of Melendez knew no sleep; in spite of storms and torrents of rain which deluged the land; the murmurs and discontents of his people; he kept at work trenching and fortifying the point of land between the San Sebastian and the inlet which he had selected as the site of his settlement, from which he dispossessed the Indians, converting their dwellings to the use of his soldiery. While he had reason to hope that the French fleet might have come to grief in the storm that had so opportunely arisen, he was too well versed in the vicissitudes of war to neglect providing every defence possible should it have escaped injury. If it did so, he knew it would return to renew the attack upon him.

Whatever his fanaticism might whisper to him of divine interposition in his behalf, reason taught him to see to it that every available means at hand should be used for the protection of his settlement first and every possible preparation be made to secure success when he should take the initiative against his foes.

He evidently studied over the situation closely. While he preached the cause of Catholicism as an incitement to his followers against the heretic Huguenots, it is plainly evident that motives of policy, or as he viewed it, absolute necessity, called for the destruction of Coligny's colony. While Ribault and Laudonniere were able to dispute the Spanish claim to possession of the Floridas his title of Adelantado amounted to nothing.

It might any day end in his being driven ignominiously from the land over which he was expected to establish sovereignty. As Scipio decreed the destruction of Carthage, because unless Carthage was destroyed Rome would be, so Melendez decreed the destruction of La Caroline.

Had they been a kindred people, with possibilities of amalgamation or absorption, it is not likely that a mere creedal difference would have prompted him to the terrible atrocity which marked the downfall of French power in Florida. But trained in the cruel hypocrisy of the age, which threw over its greatest crimes the cloak of religious sanction, he did not hesitate a moment in assuming the same disguise, and in the name of God he served the devil Ambition.

CHAPTER VI.

THE DESTRUCTION OF LA CAROLINE DECREED BY MELENDEZ.

It has been noted that Melendez had decreed the destruction of the Huguenots of La Caroline.

It was on the 8th of September Ribault made his attempts on Melendez at St. Augustine. The reader is apprised of the disastrous result of that expedition. A week was passed by Melendez in finishing his defensive preparations and then he called a council of war. Torrents of rain were still falling. The low flat pine lands of the interior were afloat, but Melendez' indomitable will knew no check from natural causes. More than any other member of his little army, he was as dauntless as he was ferocious in his determination.

The council of war was held in the old council house of the Indian tribe occupying this vicinity at the time of his arrival, a round fabric made of logs and earth, thatched with palmetto leaves. It was not a comfortable place with its rude log seats and its central pitch pine fire casting a weird gleam over the armor of his captains. But their leader recked nothing of these discomforts. He knew the people he had to deal with thoroughly; their weaknesses and discontents, the base natures of many of them and their utter incapacity to realize the scope of his ideas and plans.

He could scorn their imbecility and cowardice, but he must use them. There were no other instruments attainable and they must be aroused from their apathetic state to the work before them.

As he stood in their midst the air was filled with the muffled roar of the surf and the rush of the rain. He looked around the circle and saw no enthusiasm in their eyes. They were down-cast and moody. Already had they realized that Florida was not offering them the booty of rich cities as Peru and Mexico did to Pizarro and Cortez. Even the priests were discouraged.

Nothing daunted, he clearly placed before them the proposition to march overland to La Caroline "To destroy those arch heretics in the very fortress of their strength—in the very place which they have built as their refuge. Even the tempest, if it continues, will aid in the achievement of success!"

Murmurs broke out among the listeners. "What is it that ye fear?" asked Melendez. One arose and answered: "Shall we, left here on this savage shore, not yet entrenched, divide our strength to attack La Caroline and give Ribault a chance to fall upon our camp here, destroy it and place us between two hostile forces? Surely this would not be wise or prudent?"

Then Melendez, orator as well as soldier and fanatic, spoke forcibly and with eloquence which stirred all their hearts. He claimed to see with prophetic vision that Ribault would not trouble the camp; nay, could not, because the tempest was still carrying him before it or had engulfed him in the seas. Should he escape all the dangers of the storm and the keys which lined the coast to the southward, weeks must pass before he could possibly return to St. Augustine. In that time they would have accomplished their purpose. They would be able to turn his own cannon against him. He declared it was war to the uttermost between them. If the French were not destroyed they themselves would be destroyed. They would give no quarter; they should have none. The French were heretics and pirates, invaders of the territories of Spain and as true Spaniards it was not only a patriotic duty to extirpate them but a religious one also.

He chided them for being afraid of exposure to the elements; for being fearful of receiving a few hard knocks and loath to march against an enemy inferior in every way to themselves, because there was no royal road for them to march over.

All reasonable objections and arguments in opposition were patiently listened to and controverted with such skill that the objectors were reduced to a minority and silenced.

It was decided the next morning to prepare for the expedition which was to consist of five hundred men.

Provisions were to be carried for eight days. The force was divided into six companies, each with its flag and captain. A picked company of pioneers with axes was chosen to clear the way.

One writer says that at this point in the council arrangements, Father Salvandi, a priest, brought in a strange man partly in the costume of a sailor whom he introduced as "Francis Jean, a Frenchman, once a heretic but now recanting and desirous of becoming a Catholic, who will report what he knows touching the condition of La Caroline and will act as a guide."

The statement was made that he had fled because he had been beaten by Laudonniere. If the incident is true he was probably some thief or insubordinate who had been thus punished, for Laudonniere, as we have seen, was never a cruel man or severe in his rule.

With these conclusions arrived at and arrangements made the council adjourned. It is true that upon the next day in the midst of preparations for the march, under the discouragements of the continued bad weather, a mutinous spirit was manifested by some, even of the officers, but to this Melendez wisely gave but little attention, except to allow no delay in the preparations. Francis Recaldo, Diego de Maya and St. Vincent boldly remonstrated with the Adelantado, but his answer was an invitation to dine with him and all the rest of his officers that day. He played the part of host as well as he had done that of leader at the council, and silenced all opposition. By the morning of the 15th the army was ready to march.

They had made much of the imaginary and real difficulties and dangers of the expedition, but at La Caroline there were less than a hundred men, besides women and children, to defend a half dismantled, poorly constructed fortress, whose commandant was still too ill to take charge of affairs and was compelled to trust to careless subordinates.

The Adelantado, having thoroughly organized his little army, placed himself at its head and in spite of the rainfall which still continued daily, marched toward La Caroline.

Boats from his vessels carried the force up the San Sebastian to a point where the marshes ceased and they could reach the solid land.

Here the vanguard composed of Biscayans and Asturians, expert with the ax, were sent forward to cut a way through the tangled hammock under the command of Senor Martin de Ochoa. With it went the traitor Francis Jean, who had abandoned both his religion and his loyalty, closely watched.

Not many miles did they make on the first day, retarded as they were by the difficulty of cutting a path through the dense thickets which lined the shores of the San Sebastian, and the rain storm which broke upon them. But their camp was pitched at last in the open pine woods. Even on that night, around the bivouac fires which gleamed upon steel cuirass and morion, there were murmurings of discontent at what was deemed an unnecessary and ill timed expedition which could have neither glory or riches in it.

Melendez, however, did not suffer the least abatement in his ardor to fall upon and surprise the French stronghold, and wrapped in his cloak slumbered by his fire of pine knots as calmly as if in a palace.

As usual in this region the rains fell chiefly at a certain time of the day, coming down with such force and intensity as seemingly to exhaust the clouds for the time being, leaving the levels of the pine woods flooded, until the waters could drain off into the cypress swamps and find their exit thence to the sea by winding tortuous creeks, whose presence could be detected, as they advanced, by heavy fringes of cypress and by their closing the forward view.

The second and third days were like the first, dreary marches through flooded lands, while the rains soaked their garments and made it extremely difficult for the soldiers to protect their ammunition and provisions.

On the fourth day they were within a few miles of La Caroline, but before them lay a broad marsh in which the water was up to their middles.

It was here that the hearts of the common soldiers sank because of their toil and suffering and more than a hundred slunk away, retracing their steps to St. Augustine, where their reports of disaster to the expedition made a temporary excuse for their desertion.

But Melendez' indomitable courage, his unbending will, his presence and voice of command, still prevailed to push the greater proportion of his troops forward, in spite of the fact that many muttered curses upon his head.

One Fernan Perez, an ensign of St. Vincent's company, was bold enough to say "He could not comprehend how so many gentlemen could let themselves be led by an Asturian mountaineer who knew no more about carrying on war on land than a horse."

Even then, when so close to the goal he aimed at, Melendez was compelled to use all his skill, craft and dissimulation, enforced by claims of inspiration or revelation.

Urging them on with fiery zeal he succeeded in passing the marshes and reaching the more solid land beyond, which his guide, the renegade, assured him extended to the very gates of the French fortress.

At sunset they halted for their supper within striking distance of La Caroline, without having given the alarm. Their temporary camp was out of sight from the fortress, and as the day had been a stormy one not a Frenchman had been landward, nor had a single friendly native been stirred to bring tidings to the garrison.

CHAPTER VII.
THE FALL OF LA CAROLINE.

Under the guidance of the renegade, Melendez and his captains made a reconnoissance of the fort. Dark as the night was he soon found that it was not only carelessly watched but that breaches in its rude walls afforded easy means of entrance. Rains were falling and gusty winds were blowing. De La Vigne, one of Laudonniere's lieutenants, was captain of the watch that night, but through pity for the sentinels exposed to such weather allowed them to shelter themselves as best they could, and not dreaming that an enemy could be abroad on such a night, himself retired to his quarters, satisfied that everything was secure.

Little did he know that just beyond the range of his vision the arch-enemy of the Huguenots of La Caroline was praying that he might be enabled to change their slumbers by dawn into the eternal sleep. And so passed the night of the nineteenth of September—the last one for the Frenchmen in La Caroline.

Before dawn, with his forces divided into commands under Martin de Ochoa, Francis Recaldo, Andres Lopez Patino and himself, the landward sides of the fortress were invested. While waiting impatiently for daylight, Ochoa and the master of the camp, Patino, silently penetrated one of the breaches. They came across a drowsy sentinel who exclaimed "Qui vive!" Ochoa answered promptly "France!" but the sentinel not satisfied approached to inspect more closely, thinking they were possibly stragglers from the brigantine lying in the harbor, only to receive a stunning blow from a partisan.

The sentinel recovered his footing and drew his sword but was struck down again, disarmed and at the sword's point forbidden to make a sound. He was conducted to Melendez who commanded him to be slain, and as the dawn was breaking the order was given for the assault.

Two more of the sentinels at the outer posts were slain, while scarcely roused from their sleep. A third however, on the ramparts, saw the Spaniards rushing to the assault and cried "To arms!" Shouting the alarm he fled before them and Laudonniere was aroused but the warning came too late.

The Spaniards were in the fort. The feeble garrison could not rally on a single point. Laudonniere seized his arms and weak although he was from his late sickness, rushed into the central court and called upon his soldiers to rally to him. Some did, others were butchered as they endeavored to do so. The wild shouts of battle, the cries of women and children, rang out over the waters of the River May.

At the southwest portion of the fort some of the bravest of the garrison rallied and made a desperate stand. These Laudonniere joined and by the most headlong valor endeavored to expel the invaders. But it was utterly in vain. The Spaniards had won too secure a footing and were in too great numbers to be dispossessed. Melendez shouting his fanatical war cry "God is with us, my comrades!" led them on.

They mocked the tardy valor of the Huguenots, their feeble force, and as one by one they fell, derided them with taunts and curses while hacking and stabbing the poor unfortunates mercilessly, until no life was left in their mangled bodies.

Pressing forward through the melee, Melendez soon confronted Laudonniere but did not know him as they had never met before. The renegade, Francis Jean, pointed out his old leader saying "That is he! Laudonniere, the captain of the heretics!"

"Is it thou? traitor! Let me but live to slay thee and I care nothing for the rest!" shouted Laudonniere, making at him.

But Melendez thrust back the traitor and interposed his Toledo blade and mailed form to prevent Laudonniere's just vengeance.

As the Spaniards pressed on, the few Frenchmen fell back until only one brave, stout man, Bartholomew Prevatt, stood with Laudonniere trying to beat back the assailants with a heavy partisan. Melendez, a stalwart warrior, clad in mail, sprang eagerly forward hoping to slay Laudonniere, who, in his condition no match for him, was just as eager for the fray. At that moment he preferred to die in the battle, for so might his honor be saved. But this was denied him. A rush of fugitives bore him back towards a breach accompanied by the faithful Bartholomew. He yielded only foot by foot, parrying with sword and buckler like an accomplished cavalier, the sword thrusts of Melendez and the assaults of the long pikes of the Spaniards, his one faithful follower keeping by his side yet urging him to retreat.

Falling back, still facing the foe, through a narrow alley way, they reached the yard in which was Laudonniere's lodging. Here a tent happened to be standing around which they passed but in the melee the Spaniards thought they had gone into it and so rushed in.

"Hither, now; Monsieur Rene!" cried Bartholomew, grasping him by the wrist, "follow me and we shall surely escape."

For a moment Laudonniere stood thrusting the point of his sword into the wet earth, in vexation and despair, while the tears stood in his eyes and groans were on his lips.

'See! we have not a moment to lose, the tent falls, the Spaniards will be on us in a moment! They will catch us at the breach!" cried the soldier with impatience.

'Surely, there is where they should have found me at the first—but now!—lead on! I will follow, as thou wilt."

A heavy mist had come up from the sea and in its obscurity the two gained the breach in safety and from thence to the dense hammock was only a short step. Here there was temporary safety but they were so near that they could hear the dreadful work of death and horror going on inside the fortress and the fierce shouts of Melendez crying out "Slay, slay and spare not!" rising above the groans of dying men and the frenzied shrieks of women and children.

The panting fugitives traversed in safety under cover of the mist the open ground between the fort and the dense hammock. For a few moments they halted to recover breath, still within hearing of the shrieks and shouts of those who could not escape. Even then Laudonniere felt impelled to turn back and strike one more brave blow for La Caroline. But Bartholomew shook his head, saying "It is useless, my captain! The Spanish devils have the fort. God only can save our comrades." So shutting his ears with his hands he stumbled on with his companion, deeper into the forest.

Here they found other fugitives, some wounded, all terror stricken.

Laudonniere could command no longer, but his advice was to work their way through the marshes to the river shore, from whence they might signal their vessels at the river mouth and so yet make their escape while the Spaniards were engaged in the fort. A portion of them fearing they would be caught on the naked shore preferred to push on to the nearest Indian village, which had hitherto been friendly. Laudonniere knew, however, that this point would be one of the first visited by the pursuers and that it could afford no ultimate rescue or defence, so with a few followers he entered the marshes and hidden by the hammock from the fort pushed on through the tall grass towards the shore. The ground was soft and many muddy little creeks intervened.

Weakened by his recent sickness, into one of these the captain fell and up to his neck in water and mud he felt as if he must yield to his fate. But Jean Ressegui de Chemin and the faithful Bartholomew extricated him and stayed by him the rest of the day and through the long dreary night which followed.

Meanwhile two of the soldiers in advance reached the shore and swam off towards the vessels, still a mile off.

Fortunately for them, those on board had been apprised of the taking of the fort by Jean de Hais, the master carpenter, who had slept that night in the shallop and when he saw the fort was captured dropped down the river to the vessels, which sent out boats to pick up the swimmers. The work of picking up the stragglers was continued and Laudonniere with his faithful companions were at last found and rescued. In all eighteen or twenty were thus saved, among whom was the celebrated painter Jacques le Moyne de Morgues, some of whose illustrations of Florida scenery and native life are still preserved in the old chronicles.

They dared not go near to La Caroline, as the brigantine which they had repaired before Ribault's arrival and the bark purchased from Admiral Hawkins, were neither well enough armed nor manned to face any assault from the Spaniards and finding at last that no more fugitives were left to rescue, as those who had taken refuge with the Indians had been pursued and slain by the remorseless foe, the shallop was scuttled and on the 25th of September, 1565, Laudonniere sailed, abandoning forever the last colony of France in Florida.

After many perils by sea they arrived in England where they received generous hospitality and humane treatment.

It will be noted Laudonniere did not desert the vicinity of La Caroline until the last moment, for while Melendez had attacked the fort only with a land expedition the enemy might order up vessels by messengers to St. Augustine to cut off their flight and they dared not tarry longer, but they learned the most of the particulars which marked the fate of the Huguenot colony as the most deplorable and atrocious in the annals of American history.

CHAPTER VIII.

THE PRISONERS EXECUTED.

There are pages in history which are penned with trembling, reluctant hand, so full of atrocity and horror are they. Yet they must be written, if for naught else than for warning to the generations of men to keep chains upon the brutal instincts which, let loose without restraint, do turn the loveliest spots of earth into fit types of hell.

It was a cruel sanguinary age, when blood flowed like water, not only in the new world but in the old. An age which prated much of Christianity, yet knew not what mercy or justice or charity meant when reasons of state intervened.

It was "vae victis" to the conquered, especially if they were alien in both religious creed and race.

La Caroline was captured as written in the preceding section. By the time the sun had dispersed the morning mist the last of its Huguenot defenders was either silenced in death or bound and awaiting the will of the conqueror, save those who were being speedily hunted down and slain in the adjacent forests.

The Fleur de Lis of France was replaced with the standard of Spain and the name of the fortress changed to San Mateo, to commemorate the day on which it was taken. The arms of France and Coligny which surmounted its gateway were torn down and a garrison set apart to take charge of the place under the command of Gonzalo de Villareal.

Then came the question of what disposition to make of the prisoners. We have seen that twenty escaped with Laudonniere; as many more were overtaken and slaughtered in flight. Many had been killed in the surprise, but there still remained thirty or forty men to be disposed of.

Melendez was a man of rapid action. Having made up his mind he was as cruel and relentless as a tiger in carrying out his conclusions. He had mentally decided, even before the fall of La Caroline, to destroy the Huguenots utterly. Short was the shriving he intended for them and as terrible as it was short.

He ordered the prisoners to be brought into the central court of the fort. They were all together—men, women and children. The former bound, the latter wailing and sobbing with fear.

"Separate the women and children from the men," was his command.

"The women and children shall be spared." But they were to be kept as slaves.

"Are there any among ye," said he to the men, "who profess the faith of the Holy Catholic Church?"

Two of the prisoners answered in the affirmative. He turned them over to Father Salvandi, ordering their bonds to be removed. Continuing, he said to the rest, "Are there any among ye, who, seeing the error of their ways, will renounce the heresy of Luther and come into the fold of the only true church?"

A dead silence followed. The captives looked mournfully at each other and at the Adelantado. But in his set, cruel countenance there was no sign of mercy. "Be warned! To those who recant, the church opens her arms. To those who will not, death temporal and eternal is decreed."

Moved with pity, but knowing it was useless to utter a word of pleading for mercy to the prisoners on any other terms, the priest lifted his crucifix.

The silence was still unbroken and the cloud on Melendez' face grew still more sinister.

'Hear ye—and now say. Do you not comprehend that your lives rest upon your speech? Either ye embrace the safety that the church offers or ye die by the halter."

Then one sturdy soldier took a step in front of his fellows and, lifting up his face proudly, said "Pedro de Melendez, we are in your power. You are master of our fort and our mortal bodies, but in the face of the death you threaten, we say we cannot recant our faith in the true Church of Christ. We have nought to do with Rome. As we have lived in our Lord's teachings we will die faithful to them. We ask your mercy on honorable terms only. We cannot take the terms you offer."

The speaker looked around him at his fellows, and over their faces gleamed an answering light.

"Speaks this man for the rest of ye also?"

There was a moment's silence and then a sailor, stepping forward, spoke out: "Ay, ay! Captain, what he has said we all say. If death's the word we are ready for the end of the voyage, whatever port our compass brings us to."

"Be it even as ye say!" said Melendez, coldly, sternly, without softening of accent or show of passion. "Two hours hence these men are to be hung without the fort. Their punishment shall be a warning to heretics and invaders of the realm of Spain in all ages." Turning to the newly appointed commander of the fort, he said: "See to it that halters are provided and that my order is executed." To the priest: "Reverend father, you may talk with them and if any are converted give them your offices."

Then arose the cries of women and children as the first embraced their husbands for the last time and the latter clung to their father's hands. So sad, so pitiful was the scene it should have moved a heart of stone to mercy, but it did not.

Neither cries nor tears nor pitiful beseeching, on bent knees, on their part, swerved Melendez from his purpose one jot. Nor would he hear one word of expostulation from the priest who would fain have had more time for his exhortations, and who was himself shocked at the Adelantado's wholesale and relentless decree.

Nevertheless, he spared not his exhortations and pleadings. In his sight the way of escape was easy. But he preached and promised in vain, and perhaps, judging from Melendez' deeds afterwards, had the prisoners then recanted still they would have not been spared. As it was, the soldier and sailor had spoken for the martyrdom of all and at the appointed time the last separation was made between the men doomed to death and their companions in so many miseries and misfortunes, and they were marched forth to a huge live oak tree whose gnarled wide spread arms were dangling with halters.

There they perished and there their bodies were left hanging until the same tree bore another like ghastly crop to mark the vengeance of De Gourgues.

Under this tree was planted a hewn board on which was painted in large characters the following:

"These Do Not Suffer as
Frenchmen but as Heretics
and Enemies to God."

CHAPTER IX.
HOW IT FARED WITH RIBAULT AND HIS FLEET.

Melendez, having completely accomplished his purpose so far as La Caroline was concerned, being anxious for the safety of his new post at St. Augustine on account of the possibility that Ribault's fleet might have escaped the storm and might return to attack it, leaving a strong garrison to repair and hold the fort, returned to that place with one hundred men. The country, a low pine woods region, nearly level, was inundated by the recent rains which made the march a very disagreeable one, but the return was accomplished more speedily than the advance and his appearance at St. Augustine was unexpected.

The whole colony turned out to hail the conqueror, with acclamations of joy and a Te Deum of praise.

However, in the midst of their rejoicing the two vessels lying side by side in the harbor caught fire and were destroyed, leaving them without any sea going craft. The most of their armament, however, had been transferred to the land some time before. Attention was turned to fortifying the position, as Melendez now saw the safety of his colony would depend altogether upon his ability to defend himself on land.

The work and privation brought on much discontent and a mutinous disposition which nothing but fear of his cruel determination restrained from open revolt.

In the meantime how fared it with Ribault? The last we noted of him, his vessels disappeared from in front of St. Augustine before a north-east gale driving to the southward. All night long they battled with the storm. Vainly they tried to beat off from the shore, but could not secure sea room. The next day found them nearing the outward curving point of Cape Carnaveral, upon which or near by, finally, the whole squadron went ashore. One of the vessels of heavier draught than the others struck on a shoal some distance out and went to pieces, all the crew except the captain, De la Grange, drowning in the breakers. The other vessels were driven in upon the beach, and as the wind slackened and the tide receded, their crews disembarked safely.

Some time was passed in securing as much as possible from the stranded vessels, in waiting for the tempestuous weather to abate and in reconnoitering the vicinity.

Ribault's men were probably the first white men to view that noted arm of the sea called Indian River. They found numerous Indian villages whose inhabitants lived chiefly on fish and oysters and were not disposed to be hostile. But the country in the main was barren, except for a few small fertile spots along the river shores.

For awhile Ribault made efforts to re-launch two or three of his vessels which were not so much injured as the rest, but was finally compelled to give up that idea in despair.

Not knowing the fate that had befallen La Caroline, it was finally decided to march northward and regain that point. Nowhere could they find the connection of the long narrow peninsula with the mainland and the hard, smooth beach offered them an easy road which they accordingly took.

On the second day afterward the advance guard reached Mosquito Inlet. Near this was the usual village of fishing Indians, who ferried them over the inlet in their dug outs; a process which required considerable time and resulted in dividing the force into detachments.

Owing to the fate which finally befell the great majority of these men, few records of their discoveries remain and we are left chiefly to conjecture in what condition the shores of the Lagoon, the Hillsboro' and the Halifax were as to occupancy by the aborigines who were numerous but not warlike.

Ribault's command still numbered over five hundred men and much of their subsistence had to be obtained from the natural resources of the country; sea clams, fish and game constituting the available supplies.

They suffered most from thirst, as nowhere in this shore region of sand dunes are there streams, pools or springs of fresh water; only bear wallows, as they are called and shallow wells at the Indian villages.

The latter part of the march was the worst in respect to food; the upper portion of the Halifax, the creeks and marshes lying between it and the Matanzas being devoid of oysters. It was, therefore, worn out with privation and dispirited by misfortune that the advance division of two hundred reached Matanzas Inlet which barred their futher progress.

It was a weary and forlorn body of men that gathered on the south side of Matanzas Inlet and gazed across its narrow channel at the south point of Anastasia Island.

Its waters were too deep to wade. Sharks abounded and the tide currents in and out made it dangerous even for strong swimmers to assay. There were no boats or canoes available.

They did not know of the possibility of making their way across Matanzas neck to the mainland, and thence through the pine woods at the rear of St. Augustine on to La Caroline.

They were spirit broken, hopeless, except the possibility of rejoining their comrades, of whose fate it was impossible for them to know anything.

Their only chance, they thought, was to regain the

shelter of the fort and perhaps succeed in devising some means of escape from this land which, though not inhospitable by nature generally, had, in their case, been singularly full of calamity to them. They little knew that beyond the hummock lined shores across the strait, beyond the smiling waters of the Matanzas, winding in graceful curves between woods and marshes, a human tiger was already preparing to bathe himself in their blood. Surely had they known then, what they were to know soon, with time to measure their deadly peril and the merciless cruelty of Melendez, even then with but one stout hearted leader they might have turned the scales in their favor and meted out to the Spaniards the justice they deserved.

But it was not to be. Fate was against them. Providence had forgotten them and already their hours were numbered almost to a man.

The vine clad hills of France were never more to greet their homesick vision, at least as mortal men. Worn out with marching in the hot September sun over the beach sands; strangely red as if already stained with blood, with the glaring sea on one side and high sand banks covered with an almost impenetrable jungle of saw palmetto on the other, they made their bivouac fires; cooked oysters, clams, fish or such other provender as their scanty stores afforded; cut palmetto leaves for beds and slept the sleep of exhaustion. That night Melendez learned from Indians that white men had reached Matanzas coming from the southward. He knew they were some of Ribault's men and rightly conjectured their condition.

He did not know, however, whether the whole of Ribault's force was there or whether they might not be divided so as to approach his settlement in front and rear. He did not dare to draw his whole force from St.

Augustine, so chose sixty of his best armed soldiers and placing them on board batteaus made his way rapidly down the Matanzas. He was well aware that if the Huguenots were disposed to fight and could cross the inlet, he could not oppose his sixty to their five hundred, but with the advantage of position on his side he expected to employ, if necessary, such arts of craft and dissimulation, deception and treachery, as would be necessary to make up for the difference in numbers.

His sagacity and courage as a soldier certainly almost equalled his brutality and remorseless cruelty as a man.

CHAPTER X.

THE FATE OF THE SIEUR DE LA GRANGE AND THE FIRST DETACHMENT AT MATANZAS INLET.

Melendez, having loaded his batteaus with soldiers chosen for determined and ferocious character, from all his garrison, especially for this undertaking—one he had resolved should be at least equally as terror striking to all enemies of Spain as the massacre at La Caroline—left St. Augustine long before daylight.

The boats were propelled by skilled oarsmen and beside the men, contained the necessary provisions for a halt at Matanzas, which might be more or less prolonged by events not to be calculated beforehand.

The weather had at last subsided into gentleness and cloudlessness, forming a great contrast to its late turbulence and discomfort.

The air was balmy with the odors of flowers and spicy woods, with just enough of the sea flavor in it to make it perfection. The stars shone upon the winding waters of the serene river, their reflection rivalled in brilliancy by the phosphorescent gleams, evoked by swiftly plied oars and trailing wakes, as they sped on, bound on an errand of blood and treachery so horrible, not all these waters nor those of the near-by sea can wash the stains away in all the ages to come.

Occasionally, in the forepart of the voyage, some boat crew chanted a rude war song or even hymn, but as the morning sun began to streak the eastern sky with red and gold, silence fell upon them all.

Then sunrise came and with it the full blaze of a

beautiful October day. Stealing along the shores of Anastasia Island, Melendez sought a cove behind a hammock grove close to the inlet and disembarked his men. Here a repast was served to all and then their leader, accompanied by a few soldiers, went forward to reconnoitre. Climbing a live oak tree upon a shell mound near the verge of the sand point which formed the south end of Anastasia Island, Melendez concealed, had a full view of the opposite shore of the narrow strait and saw the Frenchmen attempting to build a raft with which to cross, but for which purpose there was little material suitable to be found. By his count there could not be more than two hundred of them. But this was too large a number to permit landing in an armed body, so taking the initiative, with a diabolical plan prompted by the evidently disheartened condition of the French, he descended the tree, emerged from the thick underbrush which concealed his force and advanced boldly alone to the shore, signaling for a conference.

After a brief consultation among the French, a bold Gascon, who was a good swimmer, sprang into the water and swam across the strait, which was not more than an hundred yards in width.

After the military salute had been exhanged, Melendez demanded: "Who are the people whom I see on the other side?" "We are Frenchmen who have suffered shipwreck."

"What Frenchmen?"

"The people of M. Ribault, Captain General of Florida, commissioned by the King of France."

"Neither France nor Frenchmen have a right to Florida. I, Pedro Melendez de Avila, am Adelantado of all Florida and hold it in behalf of Philip, King of Spain. Go back to your commander and say to him that I am here with my army to prevent any invasion of this land and punish the invaders."

The Gascon returned and delivered the words of Melendez to his disheartened and bewildered companions.

What should they do? It was true that but one man showed himself to bar their passage of the strait, but scouts had caught sight of one of the batteaus and even as they considered, the flag of Spain was displayed and they believed Melendez' statement.

Wretched with privation and broken in spirit, even those heretofore the bravest were anxious to obtain any terms which might give them a chance for their lives and ultimate return to France; so the Gascon was persuaded to return and ask safe conduct for four officers, to be taken across in the batteau, to negotiate terms.

To this consent was readily given and the Sieur de la Grange and three others were ferried over under a flag of truce. Melendez' men were so disposed, under cover of the forest, that the French officers could not make out their number when they were brought to the camp at the cove. Six well armed men only constituted the immediate guard of the general, while the boatmen attended the camp fire and preparations for the noonday meal, purposely made as ostentatious as possible.

Their leader told the story of their mishaps, shipwreck and sufferings, hoping to arouse a feeling of humanity, and asked assistance to reach La Caroline from whence they hoped to return to France and leave Florida to his peaceful possession.

To this Melendez replied: "Senor, I have made myself master of your fort; I have slain the garrison, sparing the women, the children and such as were Catholics or abjured their heresy, and have the fort well garrisoned. You cannot go there." Had a thunderbolt fallen at their feet they could not have been more surprised, and noting a look of doubt after rallying from the first shock Melendez continued: "If you doubt, or hope it is not true, I will soon convince you. I have brought hither two soldiers whom because they claimed to be Catholics I spared. You will doubtless know them. After you have dined you shall hear the truth from their lips as freely as you will."

He then retired, ordering them to be served. They fell to it like famished men—as, indeed, they were—after which the two captives were allowed to communicate with them and freely tell the cruel history of La Caroline. Nothing was concealed. Melendez' policy was to render them abject with fear—and he succeeded.

After an hour's absence he returned. "Are you satisfied," he asked, "of the truth of what I told you?"

Then the Sieur answered: "We cannot doubt that it is even so. But this does not lesson our claim upon your humanity as men who have been deprived of all other hope. There is peace between France and Spain, alliance between our sovereigns. We will be glad to leave you in undisputed possession of this country. Give us but assistance to leave it and henceforth there will be none to dispute your claims.

"If you were not heretics and I had the ships it might be so, but it cannot be," was the stern answer. "I have sworn to extirpate heresy wherever I find it. As Catholics you might have claims upon me, but you are not."

"Nevertheless we are men, human, made equally in the image of God and, if not at the same altar, serve Him also. Assist us to leave this country—this is all we demand."

"Demand nothing of me. Yield yourselves at discretion. Deliver up your arms and ensigns and I will do with you as God shall inspire me. Consent to these terms or do what pleases you. I promise you neither truce nor friendship. Go and report to your companions and give me their answer."

The four then told him, that if he would assure them their lives, they would give a ransom of twenty thousand ducats for the whole company.

The answer was characteristic of this abnormal fanatic, the cruel, relentless, unpurchasable human tiger:

"Though but a poor soldier I am not capable of being bought. If I am moved to do an act of grace it will not be your money that will move me to it. I tell you as a soldier and an officer holding a high commission from my King, though the heavens and the earth mingle I change no resolution I have made. Unconditional surrender, first of your arms and then of yourselves, is what I demand. Time passes. The boat is waiting, go."

It will scarcely be thought credible that men yet having arms, power to use them and numbers sufficient to make at least a respectable resistance, would listen to such demands.

But they did, even after a full report had been made. Some were simply reduced to apathy by despair. Others argued that it was the vigorous resistance made by a gallant few of La Caroline's garrison that had incensed him to destroy them so mercilessly. "It is likely," said they, "that if we surrender peaceably he will give us our lives."

But little time was required to determine their submission. The returning batteau was loaded with the four officers, arquebuses, pistols, swords, bucklers, their whole complement of munitions and a complete surrender was tendered.

The Frenchmen thus disarmed were brought over and with a refinement of cruelty scarcely comprehensible were given something to eat. After this they were asked if any among them were Catholics, for the one thing on earth this man feared was the church, nor that to any greater extent than to yield to its imperative demand for protection to its adherents.

It is said there were but eight amongst them who claimed they were Catholics. These were set apart to be conveyed to St. Augustine. The rest were then bound and driven in squads of six to a small glade away from the camp and as they arrived were set upon their knees and shot or stabbed, each party not knowing the fate of the preceding until the last moment.

What horrors occurred can not be imagined. But neither prayers, entreaties, groans, nor the red tide of human blood poured out upon the thirsty sands, turned the monsters from their work. Those who did it stripped the slain and acquired much booty from the bodies of the dead, over which was thrown a covering of loose sand and leaves; and so perished miserably the first detachment of Ribault's men at the place which henceforth bore the name of Matanzas or "the place of slaughter."

CHAPTER XI.

RIBAULT AT MATANZAS.

Melendez hastened back early the next morning to St. Augustine with the few wretched men spared from the massacre.

He was welcomed as a conquering hero, with all the pomp and display that was possible, even including a Te Deum and church services, so low had fallen the standard of Christianity in that dark age of murder and rapine, especially amongst the Spanish people, for while other nations of Europe had in a measure become inoculated with the spirit of bloodshed, and wars convulsed all Christendom, there was amongst the rest some humanity remaining to modify brutality.

Scarcely, however, had his soldiers cleaned their garments and their weapons from the blood of the slaughtered Frenchmen, when the watchman left at Matanzas sent word that a large body of Ribault's men had congregated in the same spot on the south side of the inlet, and were making preparations to cross, or at least were trying to, by continuing the building of the raft commenced by the preceding body.

The news created great excitement amongst the whole garrison, who were clamorous this time to accompany Melendez, being incited thereto by the display of the spoils brought home from the late massacre, and their now confident belief in the invincibility, and power to secure certain triumph of their leader.

Believing that the main body of Ribault's men were at last in his toils, Melendez selected one hundred and fifty men, the flower of his force, and embarked them as

Story of the Huguenots 75

before in batteaus and Indian pirogues or large canoes hewn from logs, and retraced his way to Matanazas.

The preparations and the embarking of this large body delayed the expedition so that it was nearly nightfall ere he reached that vicinity.

As they approached this point many zapotes, or southern vultures, were either wheeling in the sky overhead or darkened the dead limbs of trees with their ill-omened plumage. As his eyes rested on them the sombre face of the Adelantado grew darker and more sinister. "See, Ochoa, those birds are hungry for more Frenchmen! By the mass! they shall have another feast!"

It was not Melendez' intention to alarm the French until the proper moment, so he camped on shore where his force would not be observed for the night, but before dawn had them disposed at the edge of the scrubby growth near the inlet.

With the dawn came the discovery on the part of the French of the Spaniards, drawn up in order of battle on the opposite side. Their drums sounded the alarm.

The royal standard of France was unfurled and the troops gathered in martial array. Ribault, although sick at heart with the demoralization of his forces from want, hardship and homesickness, still observed military externals.

Melendez, seeing this display of determination, ordered his people to breakfast as if it concerned him not, and while the preparations were going on, promenaded the shore of the inlet with a few of his officers, as indifferently as if there were no opposing array on the other side.

Then the commander of the Huguenots displayed a flag of truce and the trumpets sounded a parley.

By the time breakfast was over the tide had so far run out that one of the French captives and a soldier of

Ribault could wade out within conversing distance of each other. The latter requested that some one might be sent over with a boat to carry a herald across the strait for a conference.

The boat was sent over and carried back one of Ribault's officers. This man was totally ignorant of what had befallen the first detachment. He related briefly the desires of his commander which were to reach the fortress of La Caroline, praying the assistance of the Spaniards to enable him to do so, promising peace and amity and to leave the country as soon as possible.

In answer to questions the envoy told of the wreck of the squadron, and gave the number of men left as yet three hundred and fifty, amongst whom were gentlemen of France well able to reward assistance.

Melendez heard him through without betraying by his looks any signs of hostility or ill will.

He must first get his enemies into his power.

"I will send over a boat with a surety of safe conduct to M. Ribault and such officers as he may select to accompany him, to confer with me as to what may be done to meet his wishes, with the privilege of returning at his leisure to his own men."

Ribault crossed the strait accompanied by eight of his officers. They were courteously received by the Adelantado and a collation served. Disarmed by this treatment, the frank sailor-soldier told Melendez all the recent events and disasters that had befallen them. At times, he was troubled by noting on the persons of Melendez' companions, ornaments, swords and bucklers, which he recognized as belonging to some of his late companions and finally hearing of the capture of La Caroline and of the advance division, was aghast at these circumstances which showed how completely his first hopes were nullified. Finally he said; "Senor, I cannot believe that you will serve us evilly. Our kings are friends and brothers in peace with each other; we wish only to return to our own country. We will leave this to you. Give us the opportunity and we will give our parole of honor on all that is sacred to all of us, that never again will any of us serve against you or your followers."

To these words Melendez replied as he had done to the leaders of the first detachment, with a demand for their unconditional surrender, but by implication at least, held out the hope of mercy.

No argument or persuasion could induce him to do more. It so happened that Alphonse D'Erlach was one of the officers who accompanied Ribault. It also happened that one of those spared from the massacre because he was a Catholic was a soldier from Lorraine and spoke a dialect that none of the Spaniards understood, but D'Erlach did. The man had served under him and was attached to him. In serving the collation, this soldier had an opportunity to speak to him in the proffering of victuals and said in his patois, as if he had naturally dropped into it, "Monsieur, laugh as I hand this bread to you, as if I joked; but take heed! Trust not this man. He means blood. There, where the vultures are, lie our dead comrades." So saying he broke one of the ship biscuits and out of it a worm fell.

Then D'Erlach slapped him on the shoulder with the open palm and laughing, said "Thou doest well to serve bread and meat together."

CHAPTER XII.

D'ERLACH'S WARNING TO RIBAULT—NEGOTIATIONS FOR SURRENDER.

D'Erlach's keen eye had noted, even more closely than Ribault, the indications presented by the trophies of the late massacre, in the hands or on the persons of a number of those in the Spanish force by which they were surrounded. With suspicions made still more active by the Lorrainer's words, he studied closely the dark face of the Adelantado, and mentally concluded there was unlimited treachery and ferocity in the soul of the Asturian. For himself he decided that he would not trust to the mercy of Melendez, at least without a pledge, and when Ribault asked for his advice he said:

"Before any arrangement is made, looking towards surrender, let a council of all our force be called."

Ribault then informed Melendez that he had with him many gentlemen of family and that he could not decide without consulting them. He therefore asked permission to return to his camp for that purpose. Consent was given to this—the Spanish general adding a word as to the advisablity of throwing themselves, without unnecessary trouble or delay, upon his mercy, he being disposed by his conference with M. Ribault to devise some plan whereby the desires of the French to leave the country could be accomplished.

With this the general of the French recrossed the strait accompanied by D'Erlach, Ottigny and the rest.

The buglers sounded the call to the standard, and with the declining sun pouring the splendor of its rays upon the surrounding waters and the sand beach on the south side of the inlet, the Huguenots gathered in a council of war decisive of their own fate, in full view of the Spanish forces on the opposite side and almost within hearing.

Ribault opened the consultation by saying:

"Brothers and comrades all, no matter what the distinctions of rank may be, you have yourselves seen, across these narrow waters, how the general of the Spaniards received us. But you could not know what passed between us nor is it, perhaps, necessary to multiply words. It all comes to this: he demands our unconditional surrender, proffering to do what he can to enable us to leave the country. In what way or when, he says not.

"I cannot conceal from you that he has captured La Caroline and slain most of the garrison." (Melendez did not tell him of the escape of Laudonniere.) "In proof of which I have seen and conversed with two of your former comrades who solemnly affirm the truth of his declaration.

"He has also captured the advance detachment which reached this point under the Sieur de la Grange a week ago, the most of whom, because they resisted, perished. This I am convinced will be our fate, if we do not placate him."

Then D'Erlach arose from the fragment of coquina rock upon which he had been sitting and earnestly entreated Ribault and all present not to place themselves in the power of the treacherous Spaniard, without at least, a solemn surety that they should not be treated as beasts fit only for slaughter, but as men and soldiers.

He told them of the garments, swords and bucklers which he had seen among their enemies, evidently taken from their slaughtered comrades. He could not give his informant's name for fear it would cost that one's life, but stated that he had been informed De la Grange and his detachment had been basely, cruelly slaughtered, as their comrades at La Caroline had been also.

"Will you trust the mercy of such a man? Look you at the vultures yonder. They circle above the same slaughter pen to which this human tiger would lead you all! Yea, and if he should spare your lives. there is naught but torture and slavery before you. For one, I say, better die sword in hand in fair battle than let the assassin's dagger have an easy, certain mark. True, it seems there is but little choice. There is no outlet this way for us save the gate of death. But if we cannot cross this strait in the face of our enemy neither can he cross to this side without our consent as long as we have arms and will to use them.

"My good sword has temper to it yet, and I will not let it leave my hand without conditions." So spoke the gallant young Frenchman, once a guardsman at the court. Such, too, was the resolution quickened in the hearts of many of his hearers. But others, like Ribault, were hopeful that Melendez would show them clemency. and so the camp was divided. Chevalier D'Ottigny finally proposed a compromise plan. This was to offer ransom and the cost of transportation to France, or if Melendez would accept their aid there were many who would remain with him to help colonize and hold the country—not knowing that the other detachment had unavailingly made similar propositions.

To this even D'Erlach consented, with but little idea, however, that the proposition would be accepted.

Again Ribault crossed to the landing to meet Melendez.

"Part of my people only are willing to surrender at discretion, but all will give up their arms and subject themselves to your orders, if you will take ransom for them. I am desired to offer you thirty thousand ducats and the proffer of service on the part of many of them if you will take them, to hold and colonize this land."

For a moment Melendez' face assumed a cruel, fierce look and he seemed about to burst out into a blaze of wrath, but, after a momentary pause, a pleasanter expression took its place. In that moment he determined to send back Ribault to his camp inspired with false hopes.

"Understand me, Senor! I cannot change the cartel, but this I will say; the ransom will satisfy my soldiers instead of plunder, and I shall be able to make your assistance, while awaiting transportation home, of use to me."

It was arranged at last that in the morning Ribault was to make a final report. As the shades of night fell, the opposing campfires glared at each other from the two sides of the Inlet. Sentinels were set on each shore. Both parties made their evening meal, after which an animated discussion took place in the Huguenot camp as to the acceptance of the proposition. Ribault, lured on by the remembrance of the Adelantado's courtesies to him, held that the proposition to ransom was definitely accepted and that therefore in the morning Melendez should be notified of their intention to surrender that he might direct its manner.

Ribault's argument in favor of trusting Melendez and surrendering, was supported by Ottigny and others, but was stoutly contested by D'Erlach, Francis La Caille, Pierre Rotrou and Robert D'Alembert.

There had been much friction between D'Erlach and his commander before, the daring and courageous Chevalier having time and again urged Ribault to more decisive and spirited action, willing, as he phrased it, "To loose all or win all upon one throw;" but as yet he had not set himself so openly in opposition.

Now, however, he felt that a decisive hour had come. He knew, that discouraged with hardships which they had ill endured; with little chance of relief coming in any shape; a large portion of the little army was disposed to give up the struggle on almost any terms. For himself, he could see nothing hopeful in the talk of Melendez; no definite promises or pledges, only the desire to get the French completely in his power to do with them as he pleased. With all due deference to the unfortunate commander he addressed the council as follows:

"Is it not enough, my comrades, that this man, who has slaughtered our brethren, will make no promise of amity? Will give no pledge of safety even to our lives alone? As for me, I would sooner trust the incarnate fiend himself than this Melendez. He but aims to get us in his power and then destroy us utterly.

"The savage has not a heart so utterly stony as that of this Spaniard! He hath fed on blood until he craves it. Mark this! You go to your deaths when you go to him. The tiger invites you to a banquet where the guest brings the repast.

"Surely we are yet strong enough, if we use our weapons, to make him concede by force what he will not otherwise. We are three hundred and fifty soldiers—why even treat with this cut throat? Why cross this strait at all?

"We still have two courses open to us. We can select some remote, defensible point for settlement and remain as long in the land as we desire; or we can retire to where our grounded vessels are, repair or build one, and yet get back to France. I for one will not surrender unless he gives us honorable terms!"

Then Ribault, broken in spirit, utterly exhausted by his struggle with fate, recapitulated his persuasion that

Melendez would be merciful; that he would deal in good faith with them, and finally said:

"Comrades, I command no longer. To-morrow, for myself and those who have decided to do likewise, I shall make a surrender upon the terms of the Adelantado; but I absolve ye all from any obligation to follow me in so doing.

"Monsieur D'Erlach and you who have protested against surrender, you are at liberty to refuse, and to do as you may deem fit. Whatever agreement I may consent to, shall not include those who do not accede to it. But before we part, and it is likely to be forever, so far as this life is concerned, for it does seem as if in neither course is there much to hope for that may bring us together in peace and safety again, let me say, that in whatsoever I have done or may do, there is no other motive than for our mutual good and to relieve our common perils. Circumstances, yea, the very elements, have been against me, and disaster beyond human power to prevent, in the will of Providence, has overruled my will."

He paused a moment and looking around the circle with a lingering glance into each one's face, he placed his hand upon his bosom and pathetically finished:

"Do you know, my comrades, that the surrender I am forced to make breaks my heart? For myself, I expect nothing. I shall never see fair France again. If it be God's will, so be it! But perhaps for you I may gain some easing of your difficulties, some chance of final return. 'Tis late; you are dismissed. God care for us all tomorrow!"

So saying, he retired to his rude quarters and cast himself down upon his couch of leaves to catch a fevered repose.

Half to himself D'Erlach murmured as he departed, in Latin, for he was gentle born and bred, "Quem Deus vult perdere prius dementat! Poor man. He goes to the sacrifice."

He then conferred briefly with those of the same opinion with him, that it were better far to keep out of the hands of the Spaniard and trust themselves entirely to fortune and the savages, bidding them to beseech their followers not to go with Ribault to certain destruction, but to follow him back to Canaveral, where many supplies could yet be obtained from the stranded vessels, through whose proper use they might even yet make good their escape or hold their own indefinitely.

Heated with the discussion, but little of which have we here chronicled, D'Erlach, carrying his morion in his hand, wandered with Pierre Rotrou down the beach towards the sea, to cool himself and watch the Spaniard camp upon the other shore.

There were still a few camp fires blazing, from around which came occasional bursts of laughter, the oaths of gamblers or snatches of song. The gaiety of the one camp, and the sullen, despairing somberness of the other, grated harshly on his spirit, and he moodily conversed with his companion as they slowly paced the sands, smooth and firm with the recent wash of the tide.

A gentle surf broke on the shore in luminous foam; jelly fish sparkled in the waters; night birds flitted to and fro with strange shrill cries; small fish sprang like birds out of the water as with a rush, sharks, porpoises or other predatory fish dashed in amongst them. After a little while, red coals only were left of the campfires, and stars reflected from the smooth bosoms of the coves.

"Truly, Nature cares but little or naught at all for any man, Rotrou, good or bad, and it doth seem to me, God scarcely any more. Look you! Over there the murderers of our comrades sleep like babes without a feather weight upon their consciences, or a shadow of stain upon their souls. To-morrow, they will thirst to redden their arms in blood to their elbows and if Ribault changes not his mind they surely will do so." D'Erlach paused and looked toward the water. A faint splashing sound caught his ear.

"Look, Rotrou, what makes that wake of light in the water off yonder little point?"

"Quietly, Chevalier! It is not made by any fish, nor is it yet a boat. A man swims toward this shore."

It was only a few paces off, and with no noise they traversed the distance. As they approached the point the splashing, gentle as it was, ceased entirely, and after a moment almost in a whisper, in French, was heard a voice saying:

"I am a friend, Antoine Uhlrich of Lorraine, and seek the Chevalier D'Erlach."

"Advance, friend, I am he whom you seek."—to Rotrou—"This is the man who warned me yesterday"— "What would you?"

"I, oh my Captain! I come to warn you again. Nay, more, to cast my lot with you for I am triste with horrors! I cannot live longer in hell!"

This he said standing on the edge of the beach with the water dripping from his naked body, and the bundle of clothes which he had pushed before him in swimming.

D'Erlach immediately saw that the man's arrival was opportune and on that account as well as meeting one who sought at the risk of his own life to aid him to save his, gave the man welcome and bade him put on his clothes and follow to his tent. Passing the sentinel they reached their headquarters, a sheet of sail-cloth spread over poles, and there, in low tones, Antoine Uhlrich told such a tale of horror as they had never listened to before, describing faithfully the two massacres, concluding with, "Mon Dieu, the cries of those poor women and children at the fort—their pitiful begging and pleading —still ring in my ears, and will forever. Poor souls, better they too had died with those for whose lives they prayed in vain! And then to see the horrors of that slaughter-pen over there, where died the Sieur de la Grange and all his men, save a few who are now Melendez' slaves and know not any day what torture he may mete to them, should they but make a misstep or speak one word wrong.

"And see! not because any understood my speech but you, for none did, a cut throat Biscayan, this very evening nearly broke my head with the pommel of his dagger, because I had made sport of their wormy bread and told me that I, to-morrow, should be killed with all my French friends, for so had he heard Melendez swear by the mass. Thou knowest I cared little for either Luther or the Pope in the old days in France, not knowing the difference, and so sought only to save my life by abjuring. But sure am I, if they have souls I have none and I would live and die with men and not such beasts!"

There was in the man's manner not only evidence of intense excitement, as he recited his story, but a feverishness arising from the blow upon his head which, to D'Erlach's mind, foretold a period of mental disorder near at hand; so he briefly drew from him information which confirmed his belief that Melendez did not intend to show any mercy to those who might surrender, and also, that he was in no condition, as to present force, to assault or follow them should the French refuse to yield up their arms.

After having had wet bandages placed on his head, Uhlrich, in a corner of the tent was told to rest in peace, for that under no consideration should he be given up to the Spaniards, and should share with them their future fortunes and misfortunes.

Rotrou and D'Erlach, it is needless to say, were much saddened and dispirited by the recalling of the miserable fates of their late comrades and the almost hopeless condition in which they themselves were placed; but they were brave men and resolutely looking the circumstances in the face, the plan of falling back to Canaveral, as outlined before, was more strongly endorsed than ever as the best course to follow.

Rising, D'Erlach said to the Breton: "In the morning, a few hours hence, Captain, see La Caille, D'Alembert and the others and tell them all you have heard from this poor fellow, whose words I believe are truth. Bid them change not their resolution, nor let Ribault and those who go with him, surrender aught except what is upon their persons. Whenever the surrender of any portion of the force is decided upon, let such exchanges of arquebuses and other weapons be made as will leave us the better ones. Bullet pouches and powder flasks also should be emptied, so that ours may be well supplied, for I foresee we shall need all our munitions in the future. Find out also how many are determined to go, forgetting not to especially persuade the best of the soldiers if possible to stay with us. My company and yours I doubt not will not leave us.

"Would to God, we had the means to cross this strait and that our men could be braced up to make one brave struggle for victory and vengeance! We could reverse upon these Spaniards the calamities and cruelties they have inflicted upon us. We are more than two to one in numbers and enfeebled although many are and worn out, were we once on the other shore, arms in hand, Melendez would be lucky indeed to escape the fate of our comrades. But go you to rest and I will make the rounds."

As anticipated, by morning, Uhlrich was delirious with fever and not capable of rational conversation. He was not violent, but occasionally he would half spring to his feet, and with a countenance full of horror, speak brokenly of some incident of the massacre at the fort—"Ha!" he exclaimed in one of these fits, "Well, struck, Captain De la Vigne! You made one of those Asturian dogs bite the dust! But there! You are down! Your sword broke on that cursed pike handle—the brutal wretches—to slay a fallen man! And there goes Laudonniere with Bartholomew to the breach—I cannot get there'"—then he would sink back to lie faint and still.

Seeing his condition, D'Erlach gave up his hope of getting Ribault to interview him so that as a result, it might change the plan of surrender, and, cooling the wounded man's head with fresh wet bandages, he ate his frugal breakfast with Rotrou and hastened to the commander's tent, to repeat to him Uhlrich's story and urge him not to surrender.

To this Ribault answered: "Monsieur D'Erlach, I do not doubt that you are prompted by sincere friendship, but I cannot believe every crazy tale that is told. This man, you tell me, is even now lying in your tent out of his mind. What he says, therefore, cannot be relied on. However, I will have the bugler call a parley and see if better terms may not be obtained from Melendez."

So saying, he called for Ernest D'Erlach, the brother of the Chevalier, a handsome, gallant youth, not yet sobered out of boyishness, but a great favorite with the General, who came quickly into the tent saluting both courteously.

"My son, take with you one of the buglers; go down to the shore and have him blow a call for a parley as agreed upon. Wait there until you get an answer and bring it to me."

The youth, with a smile, and a word for his brother, hastened away and Ribault continued:

"You have younger years, Chevalier, and therefore stronger hope. There was a time when I could share the latter but it has passed with the wreck of our squadron and the destruction of La Caroline. There are left but few with us who are capable of making a brave defence of even their lives. I see no other way save to win some concessions from Melendez for them and end a useless struggle by surrender, if he grants any."

"Then, General, I have two favors to ask of you; one is that you will not take my brother with you, but send him to me at the last, and the other, that the surrender be deferred at least until to-morrow, with liberty of action for those who are not willing to trust the Spaniards, to take steps to save themselves as they may deem best."

"Both are granted freely. And more, Monsieur D'Erlach, while it scarcely seems possible for you to ever make your escape to France, it may be so, God grant it! and if you should, will you do me a favor?"

"Surely!" was the emphatic response.

"There is in Rochelle—ah me! the fairest city of fair France—with Master Keppel the minister, my daughter, Jeanne Ribault. Take her this seal ring and this script that I have written to tell her where she may find the remnant of her father's fortune, if it should be the will of God that I meet her not again. I charge you to forget not, that she is the daughter of your old commander and comrade in arms, who places trust in your honor as a gentleman. Say to her, that her father, in his hardest straits, and if it be to end speedily, as it may, thought of her last next to his God and in dying prayed that she might be blessed with peace and happiness."

As he finished, the notes of the bugle rose clear and sweet above the monotone of the surf, echoing far over the inner river—repeated three times. Then came the answer from the Spanish side. In the melodious notes there were no undertones to indicate cold despair or black-hearted treachery, but they called to both spirits of hell and heaven.

CHAPTER XIII

THE SECOND SLAUGHTER AT MATANZAS—DEATH OF RIBAULT.

In response to the call for a parley, Melendez sent the boat over with Martin D'Ochoa under a flag of truce, as previously agreed upon. He was conducted to Ribault's tent and there informed that if Melendez desired the surrender of the Huguenots, he must modify his demands. "Tell him, Senor D'Ochoa, that I ask but little for myself. Your commander is a soldier and I will not doubt his disposition to do whatsoever he can in my own behalf; nor for my men can I expect to gain other favor, than that which is usually accorded in war between civilized nations, to prisoners surrendering without resistance.

"I will not hide the truth from you. There are many, and perhaps the larger number, who will not give up their arms without some pledge of security for their lives and the final hope of return to their native country, which the majority most earnestly wish. All desire no more than to leave you in peace. The question of sovereignty shall be left to our respective royal masters to be settled between them as they will. Here is a copy of Admiral Coligny's instructions. Call your General's attention to the fact that, in accordance with its directions, I have authority to make an agreement for complete withdrawal from this land and leave you in perfect possession if it is deemed best by me."

D'Ochoa returned to Melendez with Ribault's message. Two hours later came the ultimatum of the Adelantado.

"In the name of Philip, by the grace of God, King of

Spain and all the Indies, I, Pedro Melendez de Avila, Adelantado of Florida, demand the surrender of all the French now under the command of Jean Ribault, promising such grace and clemency as are accorded usually to prisoners. To those who will not surrender, war to the knife!"*

The herald further told Ribault that the truce then existing would not last longer than until next day noon, when the whole matter must be concluded, adding that the sooner all could be settled the better would be the terms accorded. A safe conduct to and from the Spanish camp was extended Ribault and such officers as he might choose, to dine with the Adelantado. Hoping that an opportunity might be presented to move Melendez to greater leniency, Ribault selected Ottigny, Rotrou and his trumpter, Perrault Le Bearnois, to accompany him, leaving the camp in charge of D'Erlach.

Melendez received the party courteously and made so great a show of hospitality, that Ribault was thoroughly imbued with the idea that he meant better than

---

*The following is an exact copy of the signature of Melendez as appended to his ultimatum to the Huguenots. It was obtained by a lady, Miss A. M. Brooks, while in Seville, Spain, looking over documents relating to the early Spanish settlements, and electrotyped for this book. While the Spanish, and therefore the correct form of the name, is Menendez, the French form is followed in this story as found in the history of the events, given by those of the Huguenots who escaped.

his words. Neither did the wily Spaniard fail to so display his little force, show the excellence of their equipment and their martial discipline, as to enforce the idea of his power. Indeed, the contrast with the mutinous disposition of his own men, their disheartened and demoralized condition, made Ribault feel more than ever the futility of resistance.

Every proposition of further guarantee, however, was evaded by Melendez, who fixed in Ribault's mind the belief that reasonable conditions would be given to the French upon surrender, and so it was finally decided that at an early hour the next morning, Melendez' herald, who could speak French, should be sent to proclaim the terms of surrender, on the acceptance of which the transfer of the French across the strait should begin.

Returning to his own side, Ribault made known throughout the camp the Adelantado's proposition, bidding each, however, to decide for himself whether to accept or reject.

The Breton captain was not satisfied that Melendez had not plotted to deceive them, and that evening D'Erlach and his friends held a consultation in his tent. Uhlrich by this time was rid of fever, so that he was in his right mind, and begged them not to trust the merciless butcher. "Believe him not, Captain, and you all! He has neither mercy nor compassion. His army is but a band of assassins like himself. Should you decide to trust his promises and surrender to-morrow, I will crawl this very night into the heart of these thickets and die of hunger and serpent bites in preference. Have I not seen and heard? Was ever a hatred deeper than the bottomless pit, 'tis his for Frenchmen. Give me a flask of water, a pouch of biscuit, such arms as I can carry, and ere sunrise let me go, I care not where nor to what fate; 'tis better than that slaughter-pen over there."

"Nay, friend Ulrich, we trust Melendez no more

than you. We believe he does not intend aught but evil to any of us. But it is true the General and many of the company are deceived by him, and have resolved to surrender. As for us, we will not; for he will give no straight forward promise of safety to our lives, and we believe it will be better to fall back to the wrecks and then plan some method of escape, or die sword in hand. You are too weak to march on foot now, but to-morrow shall be carried on a litter. Perhaps next day you may be able to march with the rest," replied D'Erlach, and then with Rotrou that evening made the round of the camp, to strengthen the resolutions of many for the retreat, and make his dispositions.

Early in the morning before daylight, those carrying the litters loaded with baggage and several disabled soldiers, who begged not to be turned over to the cruel Spaniards, under LaCaille and ten arqubusiers, were to proceed down the beach, followed by the main body under Rotrou, while D'Erlach remained with a rear guard of picked men until Ribault, and those going with him to surrender, should depart. Indeed, D'Erlach hoped to the last that he might persuade the commander to change his mind, in which, however, he was disappointed. More than that, in the morning he found nearly one hundred and fifty of the men, including his gallant friend, Captain Ottigny, had resolved to go with Ribault, whom surely the evil fates had in their keeping.

Sunrise came with an October blaze of glory falling on the little company gathered on the beach, at the edge of the inlet, for their final parting. Need it be said that it was sad? They had often been in peril together; had faced storm and battle side by side. It was hard to part so. Ribault was astonished, even grieved that so many would follow his leadership no longer; were so doubtful of his true judgement in trusting to the Adelantado's clemency, of which he felt assured. But the trumpets blew the agreed signal. The large bateau of the Spaniards was launched—it was dancing under the guidance of skilled oarsmen over the inlet's billows. They grasped hands and bid each other adieu.

Then Ribault, with the standards of France and Coligny and a portion of his guard, entered the boat. Ernest D'Erlach bade him the last farewell and joined his brother. And so Ribault was ferried across the Matanzas strait, not seeing the grim ferryman, Death, at the tiller.

He was conducted to the Adelantado's tent, which stood near the edge of the sand point, where it was fringed by the dense thickets of saw palmetto and stunted trees, over which towered sombre live oaks, from whose gnarled arms hung ragged drapery of funereal moss, and still taller palms crowned with great shining leaves.

Here he laid at the feet of Melendez his armor, his casque of steel, beautifully wrought with gold and silver by Florentine artists, given to him by the citizens of Rochelle; his sword, pistolet and buckler; the Commission given to him by Coligny as Governor of New France; and lastly the royal standards.

Then his companions laid down their weapons in like manner. They stood disarmed, defenseless in the midst of their enemies, absolutely at their mercy.

Then said Melendez:

"Monsieur, you are no longer a General; you have no longer the shadow even of authority in this land. My orders from my royal master are to spare none of the leaders of French intruders upon his domain—to allow no heretics to exist here, save such as recant. There is no option left but to execute those orders. If there be any among you who are of the true faith, let them step forth!"

None stirred. The order was repeated. Not one moved. All felt then that certain death confronted them. Ribault knew the doom passed upon him and his followers; but the old warrior felt no fear, only the shame of it all.

"Is it thus, Senor, that you treat men and soldiers who have trusted to your clemency and honor?"

With a scowl and a wave of his staff, Melendez said;

"Bind this man and his companions! Take them thence!"

Not another word of expostulation—none of useless pleading—did the veteran address to his murderer, but, without faltering, and with face turned heavenward, as Melendez finished his orders to the executioners binding the men for slaughter, he uttered, "From the earth we came; to the earth we must return! Soon or late, it is the same final end that comes to all."

Then as he was marched to that same spot where perished the Sieur de la Grange, he chanted clearly and solemnly, a psalm in Latin, commencing, "Domine, Memento Mei;" well conceiving in that fearful moment there was left but one source of consolation.

It was a scene, the terrible tragedy of which can scarcely in human history be paralleled; yet it was set in a frame work of matchless beauty. There was the great ocean heaving in blue and silver, its boundless bosom. The surf broke on the shore as it does now, after the centuries have passed, chanting the same mysterious anthem of power and praise and solemnity, the Creator set the notes for at the first. There were soft skies with fleecy clouds, light as angel wings; the broad river inside the green rolling sand dunes of the island and peninsula barriers. Over all, through all, and doubtless heard in heaven, swept that one human voice, singing a psalm of death, a funeral march, until the shadows of the forest closed upon the party.

There were eight men with bound hands, and to each

one a dagger-armed assassin. They were marched out of sight and sound of the camp and of their companions, being brought across the inlet in squads of ten to be dealt with in like manner, each party not knowing the fate of the preceding.

As they approached the appointed place the soldier having Ribault in charge, said to him.

"Senor, you are the general of the French."

"I was," accenting the last word, was the answer.

"You have been accustomed to exact obedience to your orders?"

"Without doubt?"

"Deem it not strange that I obey mine, then!"

Thus speaking, he drove his poignard into the heart of his victim, who fell upon his face without a groan and died. So died the others also without further preliminaries, and as with them, a similar scene was enacted, the same questioning, the same sentence and doom with each boat load ferried over to execution, till more than a hundred perished.*

"MATANZAS," THE PLACE OF SLAUGHTER

Notes of Later Discoveries

Since the publication of the first edition of this work, as the result of investigations by the author, made in the vicinity of the massacres at Matanzas Inlet, some new points are worthy of note as tending to fix the exact locations of the tragic events narrated in the story.

Heretofore it has generally been deemed that the final slaughter of the Huguenot victims occurred in the immediate vicinity of Matanzas Inlet at the extreme southern end of Anastasia Island.

A short time prior to the author's visit referred to, for the purpose of securing material suitable for the surfacing of avenues and roads newly opened, contracts were made with George C. Middleton, the proprietor of extensive shell mounds at Crescent Beach, for oyster shells in greater quantity than available elsewhere.

These oyster shell mounds occupied the shore of a curving cove in the western side of the island, immediately on the main channel of the salt water sound known as Matanzas river, a body of tide water connecting the inlet of the same name with the one known as St. Augustine inlet at the northern end of the island. Here at the time Menendez began his settlement there was located an Indian village of considerable size, whose foundation dated from an unknown past.

The inhabitants, an unwarlike tribe, subsisting chiefly upon oysters and fish, were incapable of successfully opposing Spanish domination and eventually were obliterated. This spot was the nearest one north of Matanzas Inlet that afforded wood and fresh water for camping purposes and with its peculiar topography and forest lined shores means of concealment from observation. The distance to the inlet proper is about six miles.

As the work of digging and hauling off the shell progressed, the workmen uncovered what appeared to have been originally a shallow trench. In it lying side by side were twelve skeletons, one face downward with the skull crushed. Beneath them the shell deposit contained in addition two skeleton remains evidently of aboriginal origin, fragments of Indian pottery, bone arrowheads and spear points. But the twelve first discovered had amongst them no Indian ornaments, weapons or utensils, whole or fragmentary. Several of the skulls seemed to be of pronounced European type, especially indicated by decayed teeth uncommon amongst the aborigines. Other evidences were presented in the thinness of the skulls and their facial angles.

Shortly after the discovery of this trench, a violent storm occurred producing waves which tore up the shores of the cove, uncovering a pit in which eighteen skeletons of like character were found.

It should be remembered there were two of these massacres with several days intervening and that it is hardly probable the same spot would be used for even the brutal burial, given the victims, when in this warm climate decomposition is so rapid.

The number of skeletons found in each is fairly indicative of the leadership of the two detachments of Huguenots under the separate command of La Grange and Ribault. The new light shed by these discoveries and additional notes found in old histories prove definitely that in each case the leaders of the two detachments and "the gentlemen with them" (vide the priest Grajales, chaplain to Menendez, according to Garcelaso de La Vega's Chronicles), were seperated from the rest and marched "with hands bound behind their backs to Menendez camp" at some distance from the scene of the slaughter of the main bodies, which occurred nearer to the inlet.

The priest, Grajales, was present at the capture of the La Grange detachment and prompted as he expresses it by his "bowels of compassion" interceded in behalf of the prisoners to no avail except in the saving of a few who professed to be Catholics, whom he carried back with him to St. Augustine. Undoubtedly sickened by the atrocities he had witnessed he did not return with Menendez to that of the Ribault division, the account of which outside of the Adelantado's own report to the King of Spain is briefly given by Solis de Las Meras, his brother-in-law.

That there were gentlemen of family and fortune in both divisions is evidenced by their offering in the first instance, 20,000 ducats, ransom and in the second 30,000 ducats or a total amount expressed in modern terms of $117,000. The proffer, however, of this sum instead of mollifying the crafty and cruel Spaniard served only to fix his determination to slay them and strip it from their dead bodies. It is well authenticated that in anticipation of permanent settlement in America, many of the Huguenots who joined the expedition had realized upon their properties before leaving France, what they could in money and jewels and doubtless had with them, amounts in excess of their proffers.

This fact would furnish a cogent reason for separating them from their followers, the common sailors and soldiers constituting the divisions, thus preventing his own horde of thieves and robbers drawn from the criminal dregs of Spain, from securing the richest part of the plunder. It behooved him therefore to keep the principal Frenchmen under his own eyes until the end.

Grajales says in his account that after the formal surrender of La Grange, Menendez addressed the leader and his officers as follows: "Gentlemen, I have but a few men and they not well known to me, and as you are at liberty," (although disarmed,) "it would be easy for you to revenge yourselves upon me for the people I have put to death; it is therefore necessary that you should

Story of the Huguenots

march with your hands tied behind your backs four leagues to where I have my camp."

It is not four standard Spanish leagues to Crescent Beach from the present inlet in a direct line, but as the inner shore of the island was impassible owing to dense thickets of scrub oaks and saw palmetto, the roundabout way up the beach on the ocean side and across the island to the river shore might well be taken to approximate that distance. Certain it is the distance to the settlement first established on the extreme northern end, afterward removed to the present site of St. Augustine, to which Menendez retired after each event, like a tiger glutted with slaughter, was much greater.

The Las Meras account of the Ribault Massacre is almost a repetition of that of Grajales, the same treacherous tactics so successful on that occasion being duplicated.

It is evident, also, that both accounts were rigidly censored and the truth suppressed or falsified. One single sentence in the Meras account has an unintentional touch of sublime pathos in it.

"When Ribault, the officers and gentlemen with him at the last, realized the merciless fate at hand, they arose and chanted or sang the Huguenot adaptation of the psalm 'Domini Memento Mei,' after which the General ordered their immediate execution."

Another point indicating this locality as the place where the leaders and principal men of both divisions met their fate is found in the statement that "on the morning of the 28th of September (1565) runners from the Indian village informed Menendez at St. Augustine that a large number of white men had arrived at the inlet and were seeking to cross it, upon which Menendez rightly judging they were some of Ribault's men, immediately ordered his lieutenant Diego Flores de Valdez, with fifty soldiers, to go by boat to that vicinity, with a warning to keep concealed from the French until he, Menendez, with others in his party could join them by marching overland."

The camp selected must possess not only the requisites for concealment but also wood and water. This cove was the last place along the river shore possessing these features, especially a supply of fresh water still indicated by the old Indian wells now partially filled with debris.

It is therefore almost certain that the site of the vanished Indian village at what is now known as Crescent Beach is the place where the leaders of the French Huguenots were remorselessly slain.

Bordering the bare sands of the southern extremity of the island is a singular basin, surrounded chiefly by high bluffs and dense thickets except on the inlet side, where it is fenced off by a high bulwark of sand. Within this area of possibly 100 acres, there are a number of sand peaks, one of which called Observation Mount, because chosen by Menendez to observe the French unseen by them, rises to a height sufficient to overlook the whole vicinity.

Into the hiding recesses of this natural slaughter pen the common soldiers and sailors were conveyed, disarmed and bound as they were brought over by boat loads and there slaughtered, their bones in the course of the elapsing centuries becoming deeply buried beneath the sands constantly drifting in from the beach.

Exposed as this extreme of Anastasia Island is to the full force of the southeast trade winds, with a large area of easily shifted sands contiguous, it is certain that without the pretence of burial by the Spaniards this would be so thoroughly accomplished by natural forces as to render it impossible to locate the remains with any exactitude.

The absence of other relics besides the skeletons, in the shape of belt buckles, sword hilts, fragments of other weapons, tools or camp utensils can readily be accounted for by the complete stripping of the victim's bodies by the Spaniards and Indians of every article having any value whatever.

It is right and just in concluding this part of the story of the Huguenots to say that not all the Spanish settlers who came with Menendez endorsed his conduct for while little can be found in history to the contrary, oral traditions still extant declare there were warm protests from both priests and laymen which required severely repressive action to suppress.

*Here ends the history properly of La Caroline and Ribault, although still later on La Caroline, or rather Fort San Mateo, as the Spaniards had named it, again became the scene of a most remarkable event—the sudden and terrible vengeance of the Chevalier de Gourgues.

Part II, which follows, describes the romantic adventures of D'Erlach and his men along the coast south of St. Augustine; their mishaps and final triumphs; relating also much interesting matter connected with the Indians of this region, including history and romance hitherto unpublished.

PRINCESS ISSENA (From an oil painting)

PART II.
THE ROMANCE OF IT

CHAPTER XIV.

THE DARING EXPLOIT OF CHEVALIER D'OTTIGNY, LE BEARNOIS AND THEIR COMPANIONS.

Just prior to departing, Ribault had directed Ottigny to remain until the last boat was ready to be carried across the strait.

"It may be, Captain, that Melendez will prove treacherous. Should you see aught to make you believe so, take what course you may deem best. God knows what the outcome will be."

So, through the weary lagging hours, until the middle of the afternoon, Ottigny waited, filled with many perplexities and anxieties, for his turn to come. He had kept with him, Francis Perrault, familiarly called Le Bearnois from the province of which he was a native, the chief trumpeter, the other having gone with D'Erlach, besides eight of his best men.

Ottigny had watched closely, as well as he could at the distance between the two shores of the strait, what occurred on the other side.

He had seen the first detachment, headed by Ribault, land on the opposite shore and march, escorted by the guard sent to meet him, to Melendez' tent. As the two banners carried by them were lowered, the Chevalier covered his face with his hands to hide the tears in his eyes, for with that act fell all the high hopes with which he had first entered upon this enterprise, that at the beginning, was to give to France a new world and to himself honor and distinction.

"Perrault, your eyes are as keen as the eagle's, tell me what you see," said he to the trumpeter.

"It is little, mon capitaine," answered he. "They have laid down their arms, and now the eight are being marched toward the forest around the cove, with a guard, amongst whom I see no pikes or halberds. They are gone from sight."

The next boat load carried ten, and so on, until the hour came as mentioned.

During the procedure it was noted that a number of the prisoners were dropped from the little detachments and went not towards the forest, but were left in charge of two black robed friars, and allowed at noon to parade on the beach in full sight of their late companions on the other side. These were those who were Catholics or had recanted, and Melendez, with consummate art, instigated this display of freedom and hospitality, for he made them take their noonday meal as conspicuously, rightly conjecturing it would influence the others favorably, making them more disposed to surrender. And so it did. The poor deluded wretches even crowded to enter the boat, esteeming it a favor to be selected.

Even the veterans Ottigny had chosen to remain with him, growled at being compelled to wait until the last.

They were now the only ones remaining. Le Bearnois raised his bugle to his mouth and not loudly but sweetly played a few strains of a march. The tide had recently turned seaward. The batteau was coming across the inlet.

"My comrades, one word ere we go," said their captain. "Perhaps at the last D'Erlach's warning may prove true. Should it be so, do you follow every word I give you and stand by every act. Be alert and brave for your lives and the honor of France." They answered affirmatively, and as the boat came to shore, stepped in.

As they landed, no guard met them. It was the last boat load and the boatmen themselves, escorted them to headquarters.

"You are the Chevalier Louis D'Ottigny and these men with you are the last of the French who surrender?" questioned Melendez.

"It is true, Senor?"

"You will deposit your arms here with the rest."

Ottigny and his men then proceeded to divest themselves of their arms, during which process the former noticed the group of fifteen or twenty Frenchmen in charge of the two friars, whose looks were downcast and shamefaced. He saw, also, coming from the forest opening, a number of Spaniards. At this juncture the voice of Le Bearnois was heard addressing Melendez.

"Senor commandant, I crave your pardon, but my bugle is not a weapon of war. It has been my companion for many years. Will you not permit me to keep it."

"Thou shall keep it to the last, since thou dost prize it so highly," replied Melendez with a mocking smile.

He then proceeded to put the questions, concerning religious faith and recantation, as had been done to all the others.

"I care not which you choose. Here on the one side is freedom and life, with these your former comrades, who have accepted the terms, or on the other hand the death decreed to heretics and enemies. There is no other choice."

Meantime, Ottigny, with keen eye, was watchful, though not yet fully alive to the deadly peril confronting them.

At this moment appeared from behind the tent, ten stalwart ruffians with daggers sheathed in their girdles, bearing cords in their hands and with many bloodstains upon their leathern jerkins. They were the "Matadors" as they had been nicknamed throughout the camp, the slaughter gang.

"Choose ye, and that quickly!" exclaimed Melendez sternly and impatiently raising his staff to make the fatal signal.

Clear as sunlight burst on the mind of Ottigny the whole truth. Dead in yonder glade were Ribault, generous and noble with all his faults, and all of his brave comrades, faithful unto the end, fearful as it was, to him and to their faith. The same fate was to be theirs.

The rage of battle swept over his soul; electrified his nerves; turned his sinews into steel.

With the lightning bound of a leopard, he sprang to the pile of surrendered arms, seized a halberd and aimed one swinging tremendous blow at Melendez, shouting.

"Take that, thou treacherous murderer, and to hell with thee!"

The blade of the halberd struck on the side of Melendez' steel helmet, glanced and the shaft of the weapon falling across his armored shoulder, broke off. The blow felled him, however, stunned and motionless to the ground.

With the heroic madness of the Norse Berseker upon him, Ottigny plied the stout ash shaft which remained in his hands with terrible effect, for two of the "matadors" fell with crushed skulls. His followers had grasped other weapons from the pile, and noting the rallying of the Spaniards to the tent, he shouted: "To the boat, men! Quick! For your lives! For God and France!"

Fortunately, so unexpectedly and so instantaneously did it all happen, Ottigny's party, except two who were slain by the Adelantado's immediate guard, reached the boat in safety. The one man left to guard it was stricken down. Ottigny cut the painter with his dagger, which he had previously hidden in his doublet, and with a rush the boat was pushed off, they springing into it.

In a moment it was caught by the swift, strong current, and swept out into the channel, and towards the sea.

Confusion reigned in the Spanish camp. Wild commands and shouts of rage rang over the sands, but it was too late. Their last proposed victims had escaped.

For a few moments they rested to catch their breath. Then Le Bearnois unslung his bugle from its baldric, and, standing up in the bow of the boat, blew so shrill, so loud and bold a defiance, that it rang high above the roar of the surf, the shouts and cries of the Spaniards and went echoing even to the other shore of the Matanzas river.

Meantime, D'Ochoa, satisfied that Melendez was stunned, not killed, called the friars to attend him, and rallying a company of arquebusiers, hurried them to a point near the mouth of the inlet to fire on the escaping Huguenots. But few had their matches lighted, however, when the boat came in range, Le Bearnois blowing lustily. They opened fire, and one of the bullets striking the buckle of his belt tumbled him into the bottom of the boat, breathless, but otherwise unhurt.

"Tonnerre!" ejaculated the trumpter, when he could raise himself, "a bullet takes one's breath worse than a bugle! But see! My bugle is unhurt!"

The arquebusiers raised a shout, thinking they had killed Le Bearnois, and fired another volley. The bullets rained like hail around the boat, but the latter was rolling to the bar breakers and furnished no steady mark.

"Pull hard, men! A few more strokes and we are out of their range!" exclaimed D'Ottigny at the tiller, his eyes fixed upon a huge breaker coming in from the sea. Keeping the boat bow on, he added: "Quick! Fifty feet farther, and we are safe!"

The bullets dropped behind the boat, but a great swell of blue water was rearing itself in front of them.

To capsize here meant death by drowning, or from the sharks, or at the least to be cast ashore amongst infuriated enemies. But steady was the hand on the tiller; strong the arms plying the oars, and in another breathless moment the boat rode over the mountain of water which broke in thunder behind them, and for the time being they were safe and free.

Note—D'Erlach and those who escaped with him in the tumult believed the blow he had felled the Adelantado with was more severe than in reality. It is not even mentioned in the Spanish reports and probably only intensified Menendez's intentions to utterly destroy the last of the Huguenots.

CHAPTER XV.

THE RETREAT—CAMP BELOW MATANZAS AND THE REQUIEM AT SEA.

Meantime, as D'Erlach had planned, the advance guard, followed by the main body of the Huguenots who had refused to surrender to the Spaniards, had departed from Matanzas before sunrise, to take advantage of the lowest stage of the tide along the beach southward.

D'Erlach had remained to bid a last farewell to Ribault, when the latter should complete his arrangements to begin the surrender. Even to the last, he labored to persuade his comrades to join in the retreat. But it was useless. He was glad, however, that the main body had marched so early, for had they remained they doubtless would have joined the others, for even as it was, reasonably assured in his own mind of Melendez' intended treachery, he at moments felt himself tempted to throw aside his doubts, but duty and honor called him to the faithful discharge of his obligations as the guide and commander of the little army, wending its way toward Canaveral.

Along the inner shores of the weary coast line were many populous Indian villages. He could not tell at what moment some straggler might arouse animosity and hostility.

At last he turned southward with his dozen halberders and arquebusiers, only halting at the last point from which he could scan the Spanish camp to see, as Ottigny did, the lowering of Ribault's banners, the Fleur de Lis of France and the flag of Coligny. And, even as his friend had done, he also covered his eyes, then hoarsely bidding his men to move on, looked no more, but with set lips, went after them.

It was a silent, sorrowful march. The sun blazed down upon them; shone in silver on white sand banks on one side; glittered in dazzling glory on the ocean— that great, boundless, heaving, never-resting expanse of water, beyond which lay their native land, farther from them than the infinite and the eternal.

Even in his brave heart, there was little less than the bitterness of despair, as the hopelessness of the future came forcibly upon him.

Nevertheless, he kept step with his men, nor was it long before his spirits recovered their usual elasticity.

Some two hours' march brought them to a portion of the beach where its usually smooth sands were broken by coquina rocks, with pools of water between them as the tide was rapidly coming in. Here, some sea bass were secured by spearing, and after placing a few miles of this rough section, rapidly becoming impassible through the rise of the tide, between them and possible pursuit, a halt was called for dinner.

Fire was kindled with flint and steel, and what with fish, ship biscuit, of which they had a little store, water from their flasks and the berries of the saw palmetto, which were abundant among the sand hills, they made a meal and then resumed their march; the latter part of which was rendered toilsome by the high tide, compelling them to march over the sand dunes.

As the shades of night began to close around them, some twenty miles south of the inlet, the campfires of the main body were sighted, and shortly after they joined their companions, who crowded around them for tidings.

D'Erlach left to his men the telling of what little they knew to their comrades and related what he had last seen of Ribault to Rotrou, his brother Ernest, La Caille, D'Alembert and Uhlrich, at their campfire. The latter had borne the march well, having walked much of the way, and was rapidly recovering.

To him, every incident was significant, and when D'Erlach told of seeing Ribault and his seven companions marched toward the forest, he said "Poor men! It was to their death they went, for all know, not one of those in that first boat load would ever deny his faith and that I know is the only condition the murderer Melendez would offer them."

Sentinels were posted both upon the beach and elsewhere to guard against surprise from either Spaniards or Indians, although from the latter little was feared. In this vicinity the Indian settlement lay in a heavy hummock beyond the marsh, where were large shell mounds and fertile gardens. From the aborigines the French had so far met with only kindness, and they had mutually cultivated good will.

D'Erlach found that it was fortunate indeed that Uhlrich was with the Huguenots on their march, for they were so disheartened by present hardships and the outlook for the future, that without his persistent combatting of their disposition to repent of their retreat from Matanzas, probably many would have returned even after the march began, to share the fate of their former comrades.

Fortunately, also, it was the season of the year when the climate is almost perfection; cool seawinds tempering the sunshine and driving away the pests of mosquitos and sandflies, which, at times, rendered life on these coasts a torment. Game and fish also abounded, and there was no lack of necessary food in the camp. A well had been scooped out at the foot of the hill on the inside of the peninsula, which here was very narrow, being only about a furlong in width, and from this they had an abundance of drinking water. The little hollows back of the sand barriers, furnished comfortable camping places, and palmetto leaves for bedding.

Wearied with the excitements of the day, and the tiresome marches, the whole camp was soon asleep, except the sentinels.

Not long, however, did D'Erlach wander in dreamland. Nay, it seemed to him that he had barely crossed its boundary line when the voice of Rotrou (returning from the outposts) aroused him. "Awaken, Chevalier!"

"What is it, mon ami?" he asked, springing to his feet.

"Follow me to the beach. There is a sound at sea that is a marvel I cannot make out. The guards have heard it, and are amazed."

Luigo, the Florentine bugler, who had remained with this portion of the force, rose also and went with them.

The wind had quieted down with the setting sun, but quite a surf was still tumbling on the outer bar, with crests which ran along its edge in phosphorescent flames, made more brilliant by the dark waters behind.

At first their straining ears caught only the cries of night birds wheeling through the dark, vast concave overhead, or the boom of the bull alligator from the marsh.

Naught else but these nocturnal sounds and the steady crashing of the surf upon the sands could be heard at first.

Then there came floating in from a distant point at sea, strains of sweet, solemn music, to which the ocean's voice served as the deep bass of a cathedral organ.

Nearer, gradually and clearer, the sweet, sad sounds floated over the ocean's breast and penetrated to their very hearts, until at last they swelled into the perfect rhythm of the old plaintive funeral march, wherewith the mountain brotherhoods of the Vosges and the Alps, in the days of persecution and peril buried their lamented dead.

Now high and clear, tho' distant, arose the notes as if appealing to high heaven for help of angel hands, to bear a freed soul to its immortal home. Now, low and trembling with deep pathos, the tones came over the water like the wail of a broken heart. There was behind it all the measured sound of chanting voices and instinctively there came into D'Erlach's mind the words of the psalm:

"Yea, though I walk through the valley of the shadow of Death,

"I will fear no evil, for Thou art with me."

Whatever it might be in origin, the three, warriors of proof though they were, fell upon their knees on the wet sands and their leader murmured reverently the words:

"Sit Nomen Domini Benedictum." (Blessed be the Name of the Lord.)

It was, so they thought, the last requiem for their illfated comrades, sung perhaps, by angel voices.

CHAPTER XVI.

CHEVALIER D'OTTIGNY AND HIS COMPANIONS GAIN THE CAMP.

The swift succession of calamities and misfortunes which had befallen them; their isolation in this strange land; their sorrow for their lost comrades, had chastened their spirits, and this act of devotion under the impulse of the moment, reflected no discredit upon their courage and true-heartedness. Rather, indeed, it strengthened those elements of their characters, and as they rose from their knees, aroused thereto by a renewal of the music upon the waters, they felt less of a superstitious fear natural to that age, than wonder at the cause.

"Were we not here upon this distant ocean shore, so many countless leagues from France, I would say, there is yonder a funeral barge carrying some brave warrior to his final home. But it cannot be; nor is this yet a dream," said D'Erlach.

"What can it be—ah, here comes the outpost down the beach—what news, men?" uttered Rotrou, turning to face the three who had been stationed some distance away from camp.

"Captain, you have heard those sounds which we have followed along the shore, what do they mean?"

Rotrou shook his head to signify that he did not know, and stirred up the dull embers of a fire near by, throwing upon it an armful of dry palm leaves and driftwood, which made a bright flare shining far over the sea.

As the flames shot up, there rang out above the sound of the surf a bugle call for a parley; the same with which the Spanish camp at Matanzas had been hailed.

"If that be not Le Bearnois, never have I heard him blow a bugle!" exclaimed Luigo, placing his own trumpet to his mouth and blowing such a blast in answer as awakened the whole camp, causing the astonished soldiers to rush over the bank and down upon the beach as if the foe was upon them.

Back came the answer, and then with a ringing shout, a boat shot out of the misty darkness which had hidden it from sight, close up to the breakers on the bar within the reach of the firelight.

"Per Baccho—it is Perrault! By all that's wonderful."

"And Ottigny! God be praised!"

"Hold hard! Wait until that wave breaks, and then pull in!" shouted Rotrou, rushing forward with a dozen stout, willing men to seize the boat in the midst of the breakers, and pull it on the sands.

It was soon done, and in a moment the whole beach rang with acclamations and shouts of welcome. Ottigny, Le Bearnois and their six brave companions, were safe amongst their comrades, who fairly wept with joy at greeting them again.

"'Tis as it will be at the resurrection morn," said one bronzed soldier to another. "Luigo, like the angel Gabriel, blew his trumpet and lo, the very sea gave up the ones we had surely counted with the dead!"

Then, there was indeed so strange a scene as never was before, nor ever will be again enacted on this lonely strand, backed by the unknown savage wilderness of land and lake; of marsh and forest covered plains and hills, stretching westward under the shades and stars of night, how far, how vast, they knew not; bounded on the eastward by the still more illimitable ocean upon whose ever restless bosom their keels had left no trail to mark the homeward way.

Men wept like children, as they grasped their rescued comrades' hands, or threw their arms around them in the warm-hearted French fashion. Order and discipline were forgotten; even the sentinels crowded in to give their greeting unreproved. All had grasped their arms at the first alarm, but few had donned their armor and many were bare of casque or morion.

Still higher leaped the bivouac flames, throwing a ruddy glare over the little army gathered there to hear Ottigny's story, for naught would satisfy them but to be told it all.

There were cries of rage, groans and curses even, as he told of the fateful disappearance into the forest, with the blood stained assassin guard, of each detachment, the names of whose members were whispered amongst their individual friends as if they stood by their biers. But when the Chevalier, oft interrupted by his comrades, told of the scene, which, at the last, nearly redeemed the dark Matanzas tragedy, their shouts were almost loud enough to be echoed over the weary leagues back to the Spanish camp.

The story of Le Bearnois' bugle blast of defiance, as the boat shot out of Matanzas Inlet under a hail of bullets, warmed up Luigo until with his own trumpet, he made the welkin ring with all the strains and notes of triumph, his skill and breath could call from the quivering metal.

Last, was told the brief story of the weary toiling with the oars southward along the shore and the watching for the friendly campfires, which they had hoped to see sooner. How, knowing the camp could not be far away, yet not daring to attempt to land until they knew, Le Bearnois had taken his bugle and overwhelmed with thoughts of those, who were lying stark and still behind them, had played the funeral march, to which the others had joined their voices and the measured stroke of oars.

It was a midnight hour of mingled rage and joy, in which these emotions ruled every soul with despotic sway. And ill indeed, would it have fared with the cruel, treacherous Spaniards, from their leader down to the veriest scullion of them all, had they been within striking distance. But they were leagues away; the king butcher hardly knowing whether he was on earth or in Hades; his wretched life only saved from the mighty blow Ottigny had dealt him, by the goodness of his Milan armor.

There was one among them, half chaplain, half soldier, who had a book of warlike hymns and psalms versified, such as many of them had sung when marching into battle on the hottest fields of France. Songs, born of poet souls in the Desert of the Gard, the valleys of Auvergne and Savoy; full of mystic fervor and faith, well fitted to the age and the hour. Stepping into the center of the circle where the firelight fell full upon the page he began to sing one of the most familiar.

Scarce had his tongue given sound to the first word, when more than two hundred voices joined in drowning the dull thunder of the billows breaking at their feet, with waves of melody that stormed the very gates of heaven.

Then came a prayer; with every knee bent upon the sands, of such impassioned and indescribable fervor; so strangely mingled with pleadings for Providential help and just vengeance on their merciless foes—as seldom has been before or since uttered by poor human lips.

Three hundred years and more have gone since then, laden with the lives of millions, burdened with joy and sorrow, and there is scarcely anywhere in the world, a handful of dust, a sign, a trace, or a name to recall the memory of these men, so utterly forgotten by their God and lost to all their kindred. And yet who will dare to say, they lived and battled bravely with untoward fate in vain and to no end but oblivion."

*Note—The scene here described occurred near the House of Refuge, on the upper Halifax.

CHAPTER XVII.

"LE CAMP RENCONTE FELICE"—THE VOYAGE DOWN THE HALIFAX RIVER.

"Le Camp Rencounte Felice," or the Camp of the Happy meeting, was the name bestowed by the remnant of the Huguenot forces, upon the site of this re-union of Ottigny and his comrades with the rest, and strange as it may seem, not all the sad news the Chevalier had brought of the fate of Ribault and his companions quenched the feelings of admiration and pleasure, aroused in their hearts, by the brave and successful exploit of an unarmed handful of men, so absolutely in the toils of the merciless foe, it seemed indeed a miracle which saved them.

Before, they had been so benumbed by apathy and despair as to be incapable of any attempt to conquer the difficulties by which they were surrounded, except by flight or surrender.

Now, however, the blood coursed through their veins with renewed ardor. A ray of hope shot over their dark horizon, and new courage came to them. They were men at least as strong as the eight who, at the last moment, disarmed, and apparently at the mercy of Melendez, had suddenly, by brave audacity and prompt action, broken the occult spell of his power.

So, in the morning, instead of a dispirited rabble, fleeing, they knew not where, to escape they knew not what, the whole body was ready to listen to wise counsel and to bravely carry out the best plan that could be devised.

Having thought the matter over thoroughly, D'Erlach had concluded that no attack from Melendez was to be apprehended soon, for whether or not he was seriously wounded, his force was evidently not large enough to risk pursuit and possible successful resistance. Heretofore the Spaniards had been the easy victors. Now they had wounded and dead of their own to care for. In the melee with Ottigny it was certain there were several of them slain outright, and others severely wounded. More than likely, also, affairs at the St. Augustine settlement would need their immediate return to that place.

This would give the Huguenots a breathing spell, time to plan, and, perhaps, successfully execute their escape from Florida, encompassed as it was by many difficulties.

For the present, Ottigny was the hero of the hour, and to him D'Erlach gave the full meed of praise his gallantry deserved. But his was not the head to solve the problems, or to direct the execution of plans which must be laid carefully, if success was to be attained. Pierre Rotrou, the Breton captain, was as staunch and true as the needle of a compass; the master sailor of Ribault's fleet, and put him on ship board, not to be excelled. He, too, could fence or parry with the best of them, hold a breach, lead an assault or repel boarders, but was scarce a leader for such straits.

La Caille was a brave and dauntless soldier, a good trainer at arms and discipline, a man to be trusted to execute commands, but not to plan.

D'Alembert was brave, but reckless and impatient, subject to extremes of feeling, and greatly ruled by them.

Clear-headed, brave as a lion, full of resources, skillful in planning and prompt in execution, the one man of them all to lead, direct, command, was D'Erlach, and therefore upon him devolved the care of all by nature, as well as by the rank he had held under both Laudonniere and Ribault.

Early in the morning, accompanied by Ernest, he made his way to the highest sandhill, a half mile from the camp, and from it looked over the country to the west and south. There were little groves of oak, cedar, and palms (or palmettos, as they are commonly called), along the inner edge of the peninsula, against which curved, occasionally, a creek, winding sinuously with alternate narrow course or broad expansion, through a great sea of grass-covered marsh lands, extending north and south as far as eye could reach and bounded on the west by heavy forests from which ascended the smoke of fires marking the site of Indian settlements. Beautiful detached clumps and masses of palm trees were interspersed over the basin like fairy islets.

Flocks of waterfowl, including white and gray herons, the pink curlew, white and gray cranes, ducks of many varieties, in countless numbers enlivened the waters or the shores, while overhead sailed eagles and fishhawks, the former remorselessly plundering the latter, even as they do today.

Over the little hill and dales of the narrow strip of highland forming the eastward barrier of this basin, ran billows of many hued vegetation, chiefly shades of gray and green mingled with patches of red and gold from wild flowers wet with dew drops glinting in the morning rays, while the air was pure and sweet with briny vapor and fragrance of spicy leaves.

Yet, from this scene, so fair, so full of grace and beauty, because it was so wild and strange that by contraries it recalled the far home hamlet, with castellated walls on over-hanging heights, D'Erlach turned with a sigh.

He had seen what he wished, and that was enough to tell him that this tortuous tidal stream connected with the broader, deeper sheet of water which swept far southward almost to Canaveral, and so went back to camp and called his comrades into council.

To them he proposed the transfer of the bateau across the peninsula to the creek and while they conducted the removal of the camp, some four leagues down the coast to where, on the inner shore, there was a large Indian village, confronted on the mainland side by another, both under the same chief, Ostinola, whose rule extended over all the tribal villages that occupied the shores of these waters as far as the waters of the inlet, by which they were connected with the ocean, he would explore the river. Could he make terms of peace and alliance with Ostinola and his people (of whom he had heard much good while on his march northward), he might secure such means of transportation by water as would at least greatly lighten the burdens of the march, and also establish a courier system from village to village, that would enable them at any time to get news of it, should their enemy advance upon them.

The batteau was originally a Spanish ship boat, well built and strong, large enough to carry ten men besides six oarsmen. A path was speedily cut through the brush, and as many men as could get hold of it, picked up the boat and carried it over the sand ridge to the creek, the first white man's craft that ever floated on its shallow waters.

To Ottigny, the command of the little army was given, with instructions to halt at the first village noted, until D'Erlach should rejoin him or send further orders. Arrangements also were made to signal him from the river side, should his presence from any cause be needed; and so with Ernest, LeBearnois and Uhlrich, with six oarsmen, also expert arquebusiers, D'Erlach pushed off to thread the devious water ways, leading to what is now known as the Halifax river; while Ottigny made his arrangements for striking camp and at his leisure marched southward, for the beach formed as royal a road as ever Roman army trod and the distance to be covered was not great, so there was no need of haste.

CHAPTER XVIII

THE SPANIARDS RETURN TO ST. AUGUSTINE.

During this time how fared it with the Spaniards, at the Matanzas camp? Their orgie of blood was brought to a sudden termination, although immediately after the escape of Ottigny some of the infuriated and most bloodthirsty amongst them, rushed at the squad of Catholic and abjuring Frenchmen to slay them in revenge; but the friars interposed and before they could be shoved aside, Martin de Ochoa threw his company of arquebusiers around the prisoners and halted their assailants.

"Hold," He said angrily to them. "Ye have slain enough defenceless wretches today! Because a handful of brave men have escaped would ye dare violate the sanctity of the Holy Church, in the persons of its ministers? Back bloodhounds! or by my patron saint, I fire upon you!"

The mob scowled and cursed, but fell back, as the cavalier, leaving his men to guard the prisoners, without drawing his sword walked through their midst to the Adelantado's tent.

Here he found Father Salvandi, the chief of the priests, with the help of a page, still engaged in removing Melendez' armor, having taken off the battered helmet and bathed his head with water. In this work Ochoa joined and shortly they had the still unconscious General stretched upon a pallet.

"Think you, father, the blow is mortal?"

"I think not. There is no fracture of the skull, no deep cut, but the blow was a tremendous one. That bold heretic struck not lightly. Had the blade fallen squarely in the center and not glanced off ther would have been naught left but masses for his soul! As it is, we had better go back to St. Augustine with him as soon as possible."

Still strewed upon the sands, between the tent and the water's edge were the evidences of the fray; four dead or dying Spaniards; two also of Ottigny's men dead with many wounds, and at the water's edge the boat guard still dazed with the blow that had struck him down.

Ochoa speedily made his arrangements, and recognizing the futility of pursuing the Huguenots, that very night fell back to St. Augustine with the Adelantado and the main bulk of the Spanish forces by boat, the rest marching at leisure along the Anastasia beach.

This time there were no Te Deums of praise, and great ceremonies to celebrate a victory, for though the leader of the heretic Huguenots, and many of his followers, lay in bloody graves, covered only by the Matanzas sands, their own dead—the first for whom graves were made in St. Augustine—must be duly laid away with sacred rites, although they had been but cold-blooded murderers; and their own wounded were to be cared for, besides which their Governor's life itself still hung in the balance.

For many days the sullen madness of that portion of the Spaniards, heretofore the deepest participants in the massacres, required all the joint care and skill of Ochoa and Salvandi to keep from murdering the prisoner Frenchmen, whose lives were made torture to them by their fears.

It was well for them that some petty Indian forays, provoked by Spanish usurpations and cruel treatment of the aborigines, somewhat employed the worst of the

Spaniards, as did also the erection of stockade fortifications and store houses for the new town.

In all, there were only about twenty-five Frenchmen besides forty or fifty women and children who had escaped from death at La Caroline or Matanzas; the former by virtue of their Catholicism, actual or pretended, and for their continued preservation, they were indebted to an astute idea of Friar Salvandi, by which he contrived also to secure the aggrandizement of the Church.

There happened to be amongst them two stone masons. The only available, durable building material in the vicinity, was a species of rock of marine formation, composed of minute shells or fragments cemented together, called coquina; found abundantly on the north point of Anastasia Island, the island stretching from St. Augustine inlet to the Matanzas inlet. This rock is easily quarried and cut, hardening by exposure into durability.

A priesthood without a temple was an anomaly, so Salvandi designed one for erection, and to accomplish it, and at the same time protect his French charges, he set them to work under the masons quarrying and shaping the material, even the women and children that were able, working at it. This separated them from the mass of the Spaniards and secured them better treatment. Thus, these poor people, outcasts from their native land, helped to lay the foundations and to build the first church erected in the United States, in which their ruthless, blood-stained conquerors could celebrate with pomp and ceremony the worship of that Christ, born in a stable and crucified with malefactors, whose divine teachings were ever for the brotherhood of all men, of whatever kindred and tongue, and averse to oppression, usurpation and bloodshed.

Strange irony of fate! Stranger Providence it seems

for while Fate may be deaf to the voice of misery, nay, must be, God surely is not. Yet through all this era, it is as if He heard not the many cries of misery; the prayers for help, which went up day and night from the lips of innocents, continually being robbed, enslaved, murdered, in all these fair lands of the sun.

Surely, this structure should have been a temple reared to Mars and Bellona, rather than a church dedicated to Christ, the Prince of Peace and his mother Mary, the personification of Divine Maternity, and the emblem placed upon its finished dome a battle pike crossed with a dagger.

CHAPTER XIX

D'ERLACH'S VOYAGE DOWN THE HALIFAX RIVER TO OSTINOLA'S TOWN.

The channel of the creek, although the tide was at its greatest height, was scarcely deep enough to float the boat. It also wound around over the marshy basin in such a way as to add miles to the direct distance, but every curve and bend rounded had its own peculiar scene of interest to the lad Ernest, especially. Here, a great alligator plunged into the muddy shallows, or crashed through the cat-tail flags. There, a group of cranes with long sharp bills, brandished like swords, watched in solemn silence the strange boat approach, keeping an arrow's flight away, which they had learned to measure well; while myraid ducks and herons in other places made the air roar with their pinions.

Of fish there were no end. Silver mullet leaping many times into the morning sunlight as if at home as much in air as in water, and other larger fish, darting here and there, making great swells after them through the shallows, to mark their flight.

It was a royal aquatic preserve of fish and game, little disturbed by man. In one spot where the stream touched the western hummock there were a few Indian huts with little gardens attached, hastily abandoned by the inhabitants, startled by the strange apparitions of steel capped men in a craft so unlike anything they had ever seen before. But D'Erlach did not care to land, so as the sun mounted higher they pulled steadily on. In a little while they came into deeper water, where the banks were higher, and thickly clothed with cedars and palmettos; then to the confluence of another creek, coming from the westward. Out of the mouth of this, shot several canoes filled with Indians armed with bows and arrows; spears tipped with ground shells and fish bones, or sharpened in the fire; war clubs of heavy hard wood, and hatchets of stone or shell.

They were fine, athletic men, nearly naked, their bronze bodies oddly painted, but their faces not unpleasant to look upon, for on their countenances were depicted only wonder and amazement.

Rising to his feet, D'Erlach made them the sign of peace, both hands raised with palms turned towards them, and speaking to his men to rest on their oars, signed to the Indians to come within talking distance. This they did after some hesitation and a parley amongst themselves. The Huguenot leader could speak that dialect of the Yemassee or Uchee language, used by these tribes, well enough for ordinary purposes and requested their chief man to come nearer in his canoe. Immediately a canoe with three men in it shot out from the little squadron and came alongside.

D'Erlach, after greeting the chief pleasantly, told him briefly that they "were Frenchmen, not Spaniards, and sought the way to Ostinola's town in peace and friendship."

"I, myself, will show you," replied the other, giving orders for the rest to return home, and then leading the way down the creek.

So strongly and skillfully did the three Indians ply

their paddles, chanting a quaint song as they did so, that it was with difficulty the six stout oarsmen of the French boat could keep up with them.

The creek now became broader and deeper and its banks more beautiful, with towering palms, umbrageous overhanging oaks and cedars.

As they neared a bold mound on the eastern side, covered with a fine forest growth, the young chief awoke the echoes with a hailing whoop, which brought to the shore a group of Indians, men, women and children, showing there was here a little village, although from the river it could not be seen. A mile, below this place, they shot out suddenly into a noble expanse of water,* with curving, shelly shores, coves and bays and blue woods in the distance; which, farther on, was narrowed to a main channel, half a mile in width, leading southward.

It was a scene of matchless, yet soft and pleasing, rather than majestic beauty; for unlike many other lands, there were here no high mountains or rugged cliffs and precipices. And yet, although the shores had no great elevation, the giant forest growths upon the ridges and small hills made them look higher than they were.

It seemed as if, in making their exit from the creek's mouth, they had entered a new world. Fresh breezes blew across the glittering, dancing waters, upon whose shores on either hand could be seen the quaint Indian communal villages, giving token of a numerous peaceful population. From two or three of these, many canoes shot out, evidently to reconnoitre. Converging towards them

---

*Note—Bulow Bay or Tomoka Basin, a broad expanse at the head of the Halifax.

from their several points of approach those who propelled these canoes yet were cautious, as if not knowing whether it should be peace or war.

Amused at their evident doubts, Le Bearnois sent his bugle notes in all their ringing sweetness far and wide over the water. In their astonishment at the unwonted sounds, the like of which they never had heard before, those in the canoes stood still like bronze statues pictured against the blue skies, with every paddle motionless.

Then the young chief, who was acting as guide and herald, recovering from his own surprise, lifted a conch shell fashioned into a trumpet and blew such discords as grated on the Frenchmen's ears, Le Bearnois' especially; but which being sounds of peace and amity to those of the Indians, set every paddle flashing in the sunlight and drove every boat gracefully and swiftly nearer to them. Coming within speaking distance, the chief gave them a concise and rapid explanation, followed by cries of pleasure and welcome on the part of the strangers, who joined their crafts in one flotilla, making a strange, pleasing, barbaric, gala water scene as they swept on southward towards Ostinola's capital town, the site of which was even then in view.

There were, before the voyage was ended by arrival at that place, in the convoy, not less than one hundred canoes,* made of hollowed cypress trees of various sizes, from war boats thirty feet or more in length down to

---

*Note—There is even now to be seen at Ormond one of these cypress canoes found buried in the marsh, in the possession of Captain Wardwell, showing much skill in its construction.

light fishing shells that skimmed the river's surface like water birds. It was an escort of honor, as well as curiosity, and often as they rowed along the friendly natives begged Le Bearnois to play for them. It seemed as if the tutelar deities of these lovely wilds, were in league with the player, for the shores sent back the notes with far, sweet, faint echoes, which, with the distant crooning of the surf heard over the peninsula's wooded ridges, made the perfection of harmony.

When he tired, the boatmen and the rest joined in singing the chansonettes of Margarite de Valois until tears dimmed their eyes, because of the memories they evoked of the home land and other times.

And so, in peace and welcome, came the Huguenots and their escort to Ostinola's town, where what reception awaited them will be duly narrated.

CHAPTER XX.

OSTINOLA'S WELCOME—THEY SMOKE THE PIPE OF PEACE.

'Twas the hour of high noon when D'Erlach and his Huguenots, escorted by the flotilla of canoes, reached the front of Cacique Ostinola's town. As yet, in this fair land, the evil gods had not spoken. The oracles were dumb, save only those of sweet, fair nature, speaking peace and welcome.

Halting the flotilla an hundred yards from the western shore, the sub-chief, who had guided them, stood up in his canoe, and with his conch, blew loud hailing notes, promptly answered from the shore. Then signalling for all the rest to await his orders, he paddled swiftly to the little shelly beach, which was the landing, marked by many canoes and a crowd of people, back of whom was a little plain covered here and there with palms and oaks and cedars, interspersed with gardens and many Indian houses, some of which of peculiar build, stood upon large shell mounds.*

This was the mainland side, and while the friendly herald was absent, D'Erlach noted how pleasant and beautiful was the scene. Northward and southward stretched the noble river, the like of which was hard to bring to mind, though many were the lands he had wan-

---

*Note—This spot is now known as the Hernandez hummock, near Ormond.

dered in. No artist could portray its broad bosom; sometimes smooth as polished steel, sometimes sending from its surface, rippling to a gentle breeze, a myriad shower of sun-born arrows. Its jutting points, its curves and coves, with endless variation of groves of trees and grass and flags, all duplicated by reflection in the waters; as were the white cloud fragments sailing overhead, and the sun itself in all its glory. And over all, through all, could be heard the voice of the breakers, never silent day or night; sometimes wrathful with the roar of tempest, full of storm and battle, but more often voicing the enchantment of the universal mother's nursing song.

Meantime, a multitude of Indians gathered on the shore; adding to the picture as the sunlight fell full upon their red brown faces, heron and eagle plumes, stained or painted skins and mantles, the human interests needed to make it perfect.

Suddenly, landward turned the eager faces, as the measured beat of Indian drums, mingled with the conch shell's wild rude notes, ended in so loud a shout as shook the forest and set the wavelets all to dancing.

Then Itahoma, guide and herald, stood forth at the water's edge and gave the sign of welcome. Whereat, with one stroke, five hundred paddles fell upon the water, and with one impulse the canoes moved forward before D'Erlach's men could grasp their oars. But dashing through the shallow waters, came a dozen agile young men, who seized the batteau and rushed it to the shore with ringing shouts of joy and friendship.

Men, women and children, thronged the landing. None showed a particle of fear. All wore smiles of pleasant greeting, mixed with looks of awe and wonder. Their expressions seemed to say: "Surely, the gods have come again. Let us give them such a welcome they will stay with us forever!"

Some gently touched the garments of the strangers. Some knelt upon the ground, and gazed up into their faces almost in worship. But eager as they were to give expression to their admiration and good will; thrilled through every fiber of their being with excitement; so much natural grace and courtesy ruled the host, one could scarcely deem them the untutored children of nature that they were.

Proud of the honor and distinction, their herald greeted them and bade them follow. The throng parted right and left, as he conducted the little party to where, beneath a spreading live oak, there stood a stately man and woman, clad in Indian gala costumes of soft dressed skins and brightly stained or dyed woven cloth; the former armed with spear, a massive bow and beaded quiver of arrows, crowned with a plumed head-dress, and looking every inch a chieftain, in his lithe and perfect manliness. While the woman at his side, with limbs and form as rounded and well proportioned as a goddess carved from tawny marble, seemed by the grace of God and Nature, a fit and queenly mate.

They were recognized at once by D'Erlach, from the description given by the guide on the way thither, as the Cacique Ostinola and his wife, Cowena.

The Chevalier doffed his steel cap and bowed low with all the courtly grace of a Frenchman, as did also, his followers.

Then Ostinola, handing spear and bow to an attendant, stepped forward, and, placing his hand upon D'Erlach's breast, said: "Son of the morning skies! Welcome to this land by sea and river. Let us be brothers."

Then D'Erlach doing likewise, answered: 'I greet thee, my brother! May there always be peace between thee and me, thy people and my people."

"As long as the tides shall flow, the stars sparkle, the sun and the moon measure day and night, so be it!" said Ostinola, then, to the multitude, "Hear ye, my people! These men are our brothers. Henceforth let them be as free in this land as ye are; our homes be theirs, for the Great Spirit, whose children are in all the earth, has sent them to us!"

There stepped forward now, two old men, neither infirm of mind or body, but grave and dignified, bearing their marks of age as bravely, as they had the grace and vigor of their long vanished youth. They were so wrinkled, their eyes so deep set and their garb so quaint and grotesque, that one of the boatmen, a late comer with Ribault, whispered to Uhlrich: "Surely, they are sorcerers."

"Not so, my friend," answered Uhlrich. 'They are the wise men of the nation, and the bearers of the pipe of peace."

One carried a reed upon the end of which was an earthen bowl, the other, a brand tipped with a live coal. The first took from a pouch some dried leaves, with which, after rubbing them between the palms of his hands, he filled the pipe, to which the other applied the fire. When the leaves ignited, the bearer extended the pipe at arm length to the north, west, south and east, chanting an invocation reverently, then handed it to Ostinola, who, taking a puff, gave it in turn to D'Erlach who did the same and returned it to the pipe-bearer. This was the typical ratification of the bond of peace between them all, and they were henceforth brethren.

The air rang with shouts of acclamation; drums beat; the clamor of the conch shells was again heard and so joyful and exciting was the moment, Le Bearnois unslung his bugle and blew his merriest notes. Amazed, and yet thrilled with pleasure; scarce knowing whether or not to fall upon their knees, betake themselves incontinently to the forest, yet unable to move a step; the natives ceased their own rejoicing sounds, until only the bugle woke the forest and river echoes.

As he ceased, the Cacique's wife clapped her hands and forth came from a house near by a band of girls, decked with wreaths of flowers, with bracelets and necklaces of pearly shells and bright red beads; some with light mantles of brilliant feather work; others with garments made of grass cloth or deer skins, finely dressed and soft as velvet.

These surrounded the group of Frenchmen with joined hands, and, at a signal from their leader, began to circle about them, facing in and out and changing places; keeping time with hands and feet to song and drum beat, in such a strange, yet pleasing, mystic way, as was bewildering. Each time their leader reached the point between the Cacique and D'Erlach, all lightly touched the ground with their knees. This they did three times and then vanished as suddenly as they came.

Thus did Ostinola and his people give a welcome to the strangers, crowning it with a feast in his own house, of fruits and vegetables from the gardens, fish from the river and game from the forest.

CHAPTER XXI.

OSTINOLA AND HIS PEOPLE—WHAT MANNER OF FOLKS THEY WERE.

The Cacique's house, to which the Huguenots were conducted by their host for dinner, was a large structure upon a shell mound, an hundred yards or more from the river shore. Upon the western side was an open space nearly square, surrounded by many other houses; the whole, numerous and large enuogh to accommodate many people. Upon another mound near by, was the house of the Medicine Men, and yet another similar elevation close to the river shore, served as the site of a fire beacon, whose light by night and smoke by day, could be seen far up and down the river.

Ostinola, learning from D'Erlach that his men might soon be expected on their march down the beach, sent messengers to his people on the other side to await their coming and bring them across the river so that all, that night, might have a joyous festival. With these messengers D'Erlach sent a written missive to Ottigny and Rotrou, stating that they might trust implicitly the bearers. And as he wrote it, using Andreas Le Roche's inkhorn, the Indians looked curiously upon him. So he told them that the paper would bid his men that they should cross the river to meet many friends and fear no evil. One said: "Hu! It is a talking leaf!" The messenger, to whom it was given placed it to his ear and said, doubting that it was but jest, "I hear it not. It has no tongue." Ostinola, however, bade him take it and do as he was bidden, which he did, and often afterwards, in telling of it, would say, that it was sure, "Malichee" (or sorcery) "for when I gave it to the pale face chief, his face shone like the sun, and all his men straightway clapped their hands for joy."

It is not needful to say that D'Erlach and his companions did enjoy the repast spread before them, with the kindly courtesies of the Cacique and his chief men, after their many days of toil and peril; and that between them there sprang up so strong a feeling of friendship and respect, as put away all distrust and suspicion.

After the feast, D'Erlach sent his brother to the batteau, to bring some strings of hawks bells, bright Venetian beads of glass and a spare sword, with the belt that held its scabbard.

The latter he gave to Ostinola, and taught him how to wear it; the others he presented to the Cacique's wife, and the girl who led the band of maidens, whose name was Issena, the daughter of Cowena's sister. Never had they received such gifts before, and it was a great pleasure to witness their artless delight and wonder over them.

Then they rambled amongst the gardens, by little paths that led from one to another. In these gardens were still growing, though it was October, many things for food and other uses, with signs of lately gathered harvests of maize and beans and various roots, and also great yellow pumpkins, besides gourds and calabashes of huge size, much used, when ripened and dried, for storage receptacles. There were fruit trees of various kinds, amongst them some still bearing a soft round fruit sweet as honey. Also grape vines as large as those of France, indeed, some far larger, which in their season, bore fruit nearly as fine.

"And as we went from garden to garden, and from house to house our good Cacique told much of his people's history and cutoms, with such grace of manner and intelligence it amazed us." Quoting D'Erlach further: "They were a people of medium height, well proportioned and very supple. Their complexion not so dark as the tribes beyond the River May, nor were they so savage in mien or speech. While their dialect was from the same language, it was less harsh and almost musical in its intonations. It may seem strange, but it is true, that in the speech of these people there were no words of profanity or vulgarity, such as Christian nations use. Their features were fine and regular, their foreheads high, their eyes lustrous, their countenances full of spirit and their manners were so pleasing—not to be excelled by the best gentlemen of France—that it was good to be in their company.

"Their garments, although somewhat scanty, set forth their figures well, and left them perfect freedom of action. They wore a tunic about their loins, leggings and moccasins to keep their feet and legs from being torn by thorns and brambles; mantles, scarfs and cloaks of grass cloth, skins and sometimes feathers nicely woven together; with but little difference for the sexes. Some winter robes of well-dressed furs were very beautiful, as well as comfortable.

"But for the most part, in the summer, they used but little clothing; it being esteemed no harm amongst them to go nearly naked. Indeed, it was a marvel to see how little sun or wind or rain did effect their bodies, when yet the stoutest of us would perish if we went in like manner.

"They were fond of ornaments, especially the women, who were graceful and easy in all their motions, and altogether more comely than was usual with the other Indians we had met.

"They wore bracelets and necklaces quite skillfully made of polished bits of pearly shell, small red beans as hard as ivory, large brown or black ones, found on the beach, sometimes real pearls; more often polished alligator teeth; claws of bears, panthers or talons of birds. Besides these, though rarely, small ornaments of gold and silver, also copper, brought, they affirmed, from a far country.

"When dressed for state occasions the chiefs and warriors wore head-dresses of plumes that set them off right gallantly, to which, in war times, they added the painting of their bodies with dyes and pigments in a way which increased not their good looks.

"At gala times and annual sacred festivals, the younger women and girls made much use for ornaments of wreaths of flowers and the feathers of brilliant colored birds, so that a large concourse, such as gave us greeting at this place, was truly a pleasant sight.

Their weapons for war or the chase were chiefly bows and arrows, with whose use they were exceedingly expert, being able to set the arrows to the string so fast they could be kept in constant flight, wonderfully true to the mark. Some of their best archers could set an arrow in a tree, and split its shaft with another at twenty paces, or strike a bird in flying, but not having iron to tip them with, it required no heavy armor to keep them out. Spears, also, they used, which they sometimes cast like darts.

"Macanas, or war clubs, made of hard wood, well carved—some like maces with spikes of sharpened fish bones or flint, the latter rare, being like their metal, brought from a distant section—and others with sharp edges like swords, which, in close battle, they use to cleave their enemies, as if made of steel.

"There were also battle axes made of stone or shell, polished so finely and carved so true that it was wonderful. But the two things the Cacique was most proud of were a battle axe of steel and a knife, both of Spanish make, which he said his father had procured many years before from one of Ponce de Leon's soldiers when that Spaniard came into the bay at the inlet to the southward.

"They had no idols or temples, for their god was a Great Spirit, whose dwelling was the universe, who was always near them, although invisible; to whom they prayed in times of tribulation; who sometimes answered not, because of their transgressions. But there were, they said, many lesser spirits, some good, some bad, whose favor they sought in hunting, fishing, love or war; to please whom they wore upon their persons as amulets or charms, little ugly images carved of wood or bone or shell.

"They were not lacking in other arts needful to them.

"Their women were expert in making pottery from clay found along the river shore—large jars to hold grain, meal and seeds, also to cook in, and carry water from the wells, and smaller ones to hold their paints and drink

Caseena from. (This Caseena is a beverage made from the leaves of a certain tree, of which they were fond, esteeming it to give them strength.)

"They built large and pleasant houses with rooms for many families, in which they lived without strife and bickering, for these people held everything in common; so that all fared alike and there were none poor or rich among them.

"These houses were built of strong posts set in the ground, with matting over the openings, which could be raised or lowered, as the weather should be cold or hot. The roofs were thatched with palm leaves, and open in the center so that fires could be built in them and the smoke escape. Some had upper floors made of hurdles packed with clay and divided into rooms opening on the central court. All were kept neat and clean. There were no fastenings on the doors, for robbers and thieves were unknown among them."

CHAPTER XXII.

TORONITA, THE LAND OF SUNSHINE AND GOOD WILL.

"In these houses there was but little furniture, for so fine and genial is the climate of this land, its inhabitants are almost constantly in the open air, which makes them healthy and hardy so that but little medicine is needed by them. They had couches or settees made of wicker work covered with mattings of grass or plaited palmetto leaves; also hammocks swung from post to post for sleeping; but often spread mattings on the floors when crowded with guests, whereon they slept as soundly as could be wished.

"They had a great arsenal, or house, wherein they kept many weapons of war and the chase, also trophies or rare things which they did not need for common use; storehouses well filled with provisions and the seed grain for future plantings. All these things and many more, whereof a skillful clerk might make a great book, did the Cacique show to us during the time we tarried with him."

"The land over which Ostinola ruled as chosen Cacique, because of his skill and wisdom, was not large, but had many little towns and villages in it. It extended from the headwaters of the creeks to the northward of the Huguenot camp, and to the inlet at the south, including both shores of the broad river. The province was called Toronita, the Land of Sunshine, and many parts of it were very fertile, while others were but great salt marshes, or heaps and ridges of sand covered with forest growth, or great stretches of pine woods in which roamed many deer and other wild animals.

"Altogether, it was a land well fit for men to live in; for while the forests were full of game of various kinds, the waters abounded with fish, in the catching of which these people were very skillful.

"Pure also was the air and sweet always as the breath of spring, with the odors of fragrant trees and shrubs and flowers. Although sometimes frosts came and chilly days in winter, never fell snow upon its ever green robes."

There were many months of summer, and the winter scarcely to be distinguished from it. Like their climate these people were joyous and even tempered, not prone to deeds of violent action, save when hard pressed by absolute necessity. There was so little occasion for prolonged toil and industry to supply their simple needs, that they had much time for pleasure, and nothing suited them better than to gather in their villages at stated times for festivals and dances, commemorative of the seasons or of events in their tribal history.

At such times also, the older men would recite the traditions of the past; or teach their primitive philosophy. Chanting and singing, somewhat after the Provencal fashion, by their poets, men or women, as the case might be, and the music of the flute and drum, added much to their enjoyment.

But there were times, when peril and danger called them to show the stronger side of their natures. Times that tested their courage and fidelity, in which they failed not to show the metal in them right bravely.

Let but the war drum beat the call to battle, and from every forest path would glide the dusky warriors to rally around their chief, and at his bidding do or die for land and people. Death, in the cause of right, had no terrors and wounds scarcely any pain.

There were no written laws by which the people were governed. But there was a guild of men among them, who, by age and good service to the nation, were entitled to be the repositories of the mystic rites, ceremonies, traditions and precepts, handed down from generation to generation, whose counsel was sought both in times of peace and war, and from them D'Erlach learned much of the moral code which guided this people. This was as simple as they were themselves. "Thou shalt not lie or steal or murder; be a corrupter of women, a traitor or a coward." These were the chief things forbidden. To deal with each other justly as brethren, was their golden rule.

To some indeed, much of what is written here may seem untrue, yet there is not a point that has not been endorsed by the few true and noble minded men of that time, who came in contact with the aborigines, such as Columbus, Las Casas, Peter Martyr, Herrera, the Inca Garcilaso de la Vega, Laudonniere and others who have left on record their true testimony.

The first says, writing to his sovereigns, Ferdinand and Isabella, of a kindred race not far to the southward:

"These people love their neighbors as themselves. Their discourse is ever sweet and gentle, accompanied by a smile. I swear to your majesties, there is not in the world a better nation or a better land."

Would Las Casas have been moved by pity to plead so nobly and pathetically as he did, for mere cruel barbarous savages? Or Peter Martyr left, signed and sealed for future ages, these declarations:

"It is certain that the land among these people is as common as the sun and water; and that 'mine and thine,' the seeds of all mischief, have no place with them! They are content with so little, that in so large a country they have superfluity rather than scarceness; so that they seem to live in a golden world without toil, in open gardens, neither intrenched or shut up by walls or hedges. They deal truly with one another, without laws or books or judges!"

And so, too, the son of the Incas, Garcilasco de la Vega, in his living pages, bears witness to the native, natural graces of the aboriginal inhabitants, whose feet no longer trace paths from one communal village to another, in the lands that gave them birth.

And the monster of destruction, whose insatiate maw consumed them all, proudly boasted the name of Christian civilization (?). Greedy of gold and power, the real gods it worshipped then as now, it exalted the cross, and to save souls in Heaven made a hell on earth more terrible and horrible than ever Dante described or Dore pictured.

Trampling under foot every precept of justice and humanity, it turned fiends loose upon this once Arcadian land, to blacken with deeds of shame and dishonor the records of human history for all time to come. Nay, the bloody work of sword and arquebus and lash, cutting the quivering flesh to the bone, the hecatombs of millions slaughtered without stint or mercy, are not all the worst. The enforced degradation of the descendants of these people almost to the level of the brutes, by inoculating them with the vices of inhuman civilization, is a greater crime against both God and man. And then not content with filling the measure of cruel deeds, this same civilization, as cruel and remorseless now in its silks and broadcloths as in those days of blood-stained armor, points its finger in scorn at the shattered skulking remnants of the ruined race, and says: "Let them die, for they are beasts, not men!"

CHAPTER XXIII

THE ARRIVAL OF THE MAIN BODY OF THE HUGUENOTS AND WHAT FOLLOWED.

Towards evening a column of smoke rose from the central ridge of the peninsula across the river which was a signal that the main body of the Huguenots had reached the vicinity. Meantime there had also quietly gathered many more people in the town, some by water in canoes, and others by paths through the forests, until it seemed as if all of the inhabitants of the province had gathered to do honor to their guests. Canoes were sent over to the other side and soon there was another water pageant presented, by the transportation of the little army and all the dwellers in the village on the eastern shore, across the river. It was a gay and pleasant sight as the fleet of canoes came breasting the rays of the setting sun, making a picture in the brilliant reflections from polished arms and armor—with the two banners yet left to the Huguenots, the flag of Rotrou's ship, the Dolphin, and the banner of D'Erlach—which would have delighted the soul of Jacques LeMoyne de Morgues had he been there to paint it.

There was another reception not less pleasing and fraternal than the first, after which quarters in two of the largest buildings of the town were given to the Frenchmen, who were liberally supplied with all they needed, the leaders being entertained by the chief himself, who spared no pains to make them welcome.

"This night," said Ostinola, "shall be given up to peace and pleasure. You are all my guests and shall share the best we have. Tomorrow, if it pleases you, we will meet in council, and whatsoever you decide it shall be done. See! Here comes my best hunters, and the Great Spirit has deigned to smile upon them!"

There came a party, some carrying between them a great bear, the arrows wherewith it had been slain still sticking in it; others carrying deer, wild turkey, other game and fish, so plentiful indeed, that with the stores at hand there was no dearth with any. Never were the Frenchmen better regaled, and though the remembrance of their misfortunes was still fresh upon them, the kindness and good will shown by Ostinola and his people cheered their very hearts.

That night the central square was lighted with torches and after the Indians, under the leadership of their chiefs, had made a display of their national ceremonies, illustrating their skill in war and hunting; engaged in weird but pleasing mystic rites, whereby they signified the completion of the bond of brotherhood between them; the Frenchmen in their turn, with the trumpeters, Le Bearnois and Luigo, also some mandolin players, who had kept their instruments through all their difficulties, to make music for them—undertook to teach the French way of dancing and merry-making to their red friends, whereat they all enjoyed themselves right royally.

It was not difficult indeed with pupils so full of grace and suppleness naturally as the forest maidens were, to teach them how to do their parts as well or even better than their white sisters might have done. Nay, for many years thereafter, there were some, who, over their tankards under the vine-clad arbors of their native land, told how the younger brother of their leader, with the Princess Issena, led a dance the like of which for grace and beauty was never seen at the King's court.

So well fared the whole band of Huguenots, that they besought their leaders to let them tarry awhile in Toronita and rest themselves, and seeing that they had much need of it to brace them for the hardships yet to come, D'Erlach presented their petition to Ostinola, who was as greatly pleased to grant it as they had desire for it. So, when the festival ended at a late hour, the trumpeters called attention and a proclamation was made, that on the morrow, which was the last day of the week, they all should have perfect freedom so that they stayed within bugle call, while a council would be held with their new friends and allies to settle on the future plan of action. Caution was also given that they were in no wise to do aught by word or deed that might offend, for such as did so far forget their duty and honor, as to forfeit the good will of their hosts, should be severely punished; which warning proved to be needless.

At the council were present, besides the leaders of the Huguenots, Ostinola, Itahoma and a number of other chiefs and head men, renowned for valor and discretion; to whom D'Erlach concisely recounted their condition and all the events preceding. While he spoke there was grave silence amongst them all, though many glances of intelligence passed between them, showing that the main facts were already known to them. Especially was this the case when he told of the cruel, treacherous character of the Spaniards and their atrocious deeds. "As for himself and his followers there was no choice but to face their foes sword in hand and give them battle, trusting in the God of right and justice for victory and deliverance."

"I doubt not my friends, that it will not be long ere the Spaniard seeks to set his iron heel upon you, as he did upon my dead brethren, who had harmed him not. We came as friends across the great waters and landing first upon your shores sought but to make for ourselves a peaceful home. The Spaniards came, not only to destroy us, but to take from you your lands and liberties, as they have done wherever their feet have trodden. Will you permit it? Will you turn your friends away and folding your hands let these robbers and murderers work their will? I trow not! Though they have many great ships that sail the seas and pour forth thunder from their sides, and they are clad in armor that will turn or break many an arrow shaft. The odds may be great against you, and were there any safe course for you to avoid conflict with them, I would say take it and let us go, but there is not."

Then uprose the oldest man among them and clearly recited the tales of former Spanish invasion and how despite their armor, their cannon, their arquebuses and swords of keen shining metal, they had at last left but their bones to whiten the land they came to conquer.

Lastly, Ostinola addressed them, showing that wisdom and judgement, which made him see the peril for the future for which he was renowned, but displaying the fearless courage of the hero ready to face all dangers.

The conclusion arrived at was that D'Erlach and such of his men as chose, should stay with them to help drive back the Spaniards, if they came, while the rest should be assisted on their return to the wrecks, for which purpose a fleet of canoes should be detailed, chiefly to carry provisions to supply them while they worked to build or repair a vessel, and returning bring back arms and material useful to repel the expected invasion, which was not long in coming.

CHAPTER XXIV

HOW CACIQUE OSTINOLA ENTERTAINED THE HUGUENOTS—THE BATTLE OF MATANZAS.

It was no small task which the Cacique took upon himself to entertain his guests, but it was one in which all the people gladly joined.

To old and young alike, it seemed a festal occasion and there was naught which they could do to give the Huguenots rest, refreshment and pleasure, that they did not.

There were boating and fishing parties upon the water; some went with the hunters and scoured the adjacent forests; others mended their garments or washed them, polished their weapons and such armor as they wore; and even those who were sick or wearied with their hardships, under the gentle ministration tendered with open hands and warm hearts, rapidly recovered their spirits.

Of all the people who have landed in the past times on American shores, the French, whether Protestant or Catholic, stand first in humane treatment of the aborigines and in the readiness with which they fraternized with them. This is true of them, whether tracking the snows of the North or striving to plant their colonies in the sunny Southland.

Sunday, while not rigidly kept by all the Huguenots as a day of worship, had its simple yet impressive services, to witness and participate in which, all the army and the people gathered in the shade of the great live oaks, under one of which was erected a stand for their preacher—the same who led the thanksgiving at Le Camp Renconte Felice—Andreas Le Roche. His text was David's prayer that God would revenge him on his foes. The Indians, although they comprehended but little, behaved in a most exemplary manner, believing rightly that it was a sacred ceremony of their white friends.

Four days the little army tarried in Toronita and then a fleet of canoes having been gathered for the purpose, with Indian oarsmen under Itahoma, the main body in charge of Rotrou, embarked to proceed as far as they could by water on the return to Canaveral; D'Erlach remaining with thirty men to watch the Spanish advance and aid Ostinola to prepare against aggression.

Ten days after, Itahoma returned with such military and other supplies as were needed, especially of clothing; the Indians at Canaveral in whose charge everything had been left, having carefully and faithfully discharged their trust. There were a number of pikes and battleaxes given to Ostinola with which to arm a portion of his warriors.

On the 10th of November, a courier from the northern settlement came in, with the report that fifty armed Spaniards had landed at Matanzas and were engaged in building a stockade fort, from which annoying scouting parties would doubtless be sent forth.

To prevent this, D'Erlach with his men and Ostinola with two hundred Indians, immediately departed for the head of the river by canoe, the water way enabling them to get within a short distance of the enemy.

That night, they camped in a hummock less than a

league from Matanzas and sent out scouts to ascertain and report concerning the Spaniards.

They confirmed the statements of the courier, and so at dawn the little army of allies moved upon the enemy. The Spanish sentinels were alert, and as the Frenchmen in the van emerged into the open space cleared for the stockade, fired their arquebuses and fell back to the camp. Le Bearnois' bugle blew the charge. Fierce war cries echoed far and wide. A flight of arrows filled the air, falling like stinging hail upon the Spaniards, followed by a volley from the French arquebuses. "Drop your arquebuses, my men, and charge these murderers of your comrades with pike and halberd! To close quarters and strike home!" commanded D'Erlach, himself leading the way.

Confused somewhat, as they were, by the sudden attack, the Spaniards yet rallied manfully to the defense; and in a moment the little grove of trees in which they had encamped, bordering the Matanzas, rang with scattering shots of arquebuses, the clash of steel on steel, and the war cries of the combatants.

Unused to firearms, and little used to hand-to-hand fighting, it required all of Ostinola's influence to keep his followers from flight, but, armed with only a buckler for armor, he threw himself into the hottest of the fray as gallantly as D'Erlach himself, and so shouting their wild war cries, they from emulation kept pace with him, although never in all their lives had they faced such terrible foes.

Compelled to desert the camp itself by the fierce onslaught of their foes, the Spaniards, commanded by Fernan Perez, fell back to the landing behind piles of timber accumulated for the stockade and there made a stubborn defense. Side by side with D'Erlach was Uhlrich, and in the close contest more than once, his halberd turned aside the spear point thrust at his leader, to be requited in turn by the dexterous sword play of the Chevalier.

To both, it seemed this day, as if danger and desperate peril of death were joy, for they were now meeting their deadly enemies on equal terms, and were determined on revenge for La Caroline and Ribault's slaughter.

In one of the passage ways between the piles of timber, these two met Perez and a stalwart Biscayan, whom Uhlrich recognized as the one whose dagger blow had been so nearly fatal to him.

"Deal thou with Fernan Perez, Chevalier!" said Uhlrich. "Here's at thee, thou dog of an assassin, Diego Diaz!" For he was one of the "Matadors" whose hands were so lately red with the blood of Ribault and his comrades. Throwing aside their pikes as too clumsy for such close quarters, Uhlrich and Diaz closed with one another so fiercely that it was a wonder both were not disabled at the first charge.

Meantime D'Erlach and Perez also came within sword reach of each other. Both were skillful swordsmen. Sometimes above their heads flashed the glittering steel in air, meeting and clashing together, or glancing off buckler and steel cap, or deadly thrust met counter guard.

The Spaniard's sword was heaviest, but the French man more than made up the difference in weight of metal by the superb skill with which he handled his weapon.

In the very midst of the fight, five of six of the Spaniards ran to the landing, where was a culverin intended for the stockade when it should be completed, and hastened to load it and train it upon this very gap, now the center of attack.

"Bid Ostinola's archers send their heaviest volleys of arrows on the culverin party!" shouted D'Erlach to one of his men, standing on the defensive for a moment.

This emboldened Perez, who, making a tremendous assault with his sword point which D'Erlach caught upon his buckler, left his side exposed and in a moment was transfixed by his opponent's blade; over his body fell that of Diaz, and as the two went down, there arose cries from the Spaniards to retreat to the boats.

The Spaniards now were desperately pressed. They realized the day was lost and all that could be done was to save themselves as best they might. Sullenly, those left of them unhurt, formed a rear guard to hold their assailants in check, while the wounded got aboard the boats; then they pulled out into the stream followed by arrows, bullets, and loud shouts of triumph from the victors. Eight of their number, including their leader, were killed outright, four were left as prisoners, and many of those who had escaped on the boats were more or less severely wounded.

On the other hand not one of the Frenchmen had been killed, although several were wounded, but none seriously. The Indians had suffered more severely, losing several killed and more wounded, their mishaps coming chiefly from their lack of skill and knowledge and reckless courage, after they were once aroused to battle.

CHAPTER XXV.

THE ALLIES GAIN A VICTORY—THE BURIAL OF THE WARRIORS.

It was with grim satisfaction that the Huguenots, at last the victors in a fair combat with their enemies, proceeded to gather up the provisions, material and munitions left behind by the flying Spaniards, first caring for their wounded as well as their appliances permitted and then burying the dead Spaniards; after which they threw the culverin into the river and fired the piles of stockade timber, enough of which was reserved to lash into a raft that would serve to carry the four prisoners across the strait; for on investigation it was found they were not implicated, directly or indirectly, in the late massacres, being arrivals on one of Melendez' belated vessels; so after taking their parole on oath, they were sent across to Anastasia Island, to find their way to St. Augustine as best they could.

Some of the Huguenots were indignant at their release, claiming that no Spaniards should have mercy shown them for they gave none. But the word of their commander sufficed to bring them to the side of clemency, and so the prisoners were released, with a message to Melendez, forbidding any further invasions into the territory of Ostinola. "For," said D'Erlach to them, "should your treacherous master send any more of his assassins and robbers into this country, by the help of God and my good sword, they shall be even as these eight are whom you leave behind. Go now! And thank God that you fell into the hands of men, whom you call heretics, but who are not such barbarians as the Spaniards."

Thus mercifully dealt this leader of the Huguenots with his disarmed defenseless enemies, in sight of the very spot where Melendez and his men had basely and cruelly slaughtered his comrades. Not from motives of policy or with any hope of modifying the relentless, cruel disposition of the Adelantado; not even from the desire to show that Frenchmen were more noble-hearted than the Spaniards, but for humanity's sake.

Whatever was the true reason; race, religion, or the better appreciation of the fundamental principles of humanity, which the French have more commonly shown than their neighbors; inured as he was, with all men of that age, to scenes of carnage and battle; ready at what he deemed to be the call of duty or honor, to throw himself into the thickest of the fray at a moment's notice, D'Erlach was equally ready after the conflict was over to respond to the voice of mercy.

Having disposed of the Spaniards, dead and living, there occurred another event which may be of sufficient interest to describe.

THE BURIAL OF THE WARRIORS.

Three of the Indians had been killed in the attack; a fourth was mortally wounded and in a few hours died surrounded by his companions, chanting until his lips stiffened and could no more give utterance to the words, the immemorial death song of the aborigines.

Then the chief took the warrior's bow, snapped the bow string and placed it upon his breast, folding his arms over it as had been done with the others. Biers were made of crossed spears and the bodies were carried a little way southward along the river to a high knoll, overlooking its basin, whose summit was first cleaned of grass and shrubs, then leveled and covered with a layer of moss and leaves, upon which the four bodies were arranged with their heads to the center, marked by a coquina stone.

Then led by the Cacique himself, the whole band marched and counter-marched around the place of burial, to the measured cadence of a funeral chant, timed by war drums, but not so loud as to drown the wail of human voices, mingling with the solemn sound of the not distant surf; a most fitting and impressive accompaniment to these last services, bestowed upon the dead by their living comrades. This finished, Ostinola stepped inside the circle, and like one calling the roll of a company, spoke the four dead men's names, pausing each time as if for answer, then he said:

"Behold, my brethren, these men answer not the call of their chieftain! The day is far spent, yet they sleep. I cannot arouse them by speaking their names."

"Listen! I will call them to the chase! Join me in the hunters' cry!" Then the air resounded with such cries as the Indians are wont to make when they have brought the game to bay and send upon it a shower of arrows.

"They stir not! They answer not! Deep is the spell of the sleep god upon them. Once more will I strive to awaken them. If there be any spirit in them they will arise—Men of Toronita, let the war drums sound! Give voice to the war cry! The foe is here!"

So said, so done! Out over the sand dunes and valleys rang the combined sounds, making the leaves tremble; startling the eagles and ospreys overhead; dying in faint echoes against the fronts of the far hummocks and when silence came, again Ostinola spoke.

"These were good men and true. Never before have they failed to answer the summons to the chase or battle. It is because they cannot. Not sloth, nor sleep, nor fear hold them back. Their quivers are empty, their bow strings are broken. Their spirits are in that land from whence none ever return, save in dreams and visions. They have died in battling bravely to drive back the enemy from their native land. They have won rest and happiness in the land of spirits. Peace be with them evermore."

Then a covering of moss and leaves was placed over the dead warriors. Earth and shell heaped upon them, to this day marking their burial place with grass and flowers, more enduring than the marble shaft gnawed by the tooth of Time, overthrown by earthquake, or shattered by lightning.

CHAPTER XXVI

THE RETURN—ERNEST AND ESSENA—THE STORY THAT IS OLD, BUT EVER NEW.

The Huguenots joined with the Indians in their funeral rites, for already so close was their community of interests and sympathies, the narrow confines of creeds did not separate them. This they did, led by their chaplain, Le Roche, standing with uncovered heads, while he commended the souls of the slain to the keeping of the Almighty. Then, laden with the spoils of the Spaniards, which were not inconsiderable, they retraced their steps to the camp and from thence on the next day returned to Ostinola's town where they were received with great rejoicing, although there was sorrow for the four brave warriors who had lost their lives, especially on the part of their wives and children.

In accordance with their custom on such occasions, the women retired together to a building called the house of sorrow and there fasted and mourned for the dead three days; after which they resumed their usual duties, receiving many tokens of respect and affection as widows of distinguished warriors, while their children were solemnly adopted as wards of the nation.

In such respects, these poor savages, could well teach a lesson to the civilized nations which too often utterly fail to recognize the patriotic sacrifices made in their defense, or if they do in a measure remember them, it is by piling up monuments of marble and giving to the widows and orphans the fragments chipped from the original blocks instead of bread.

From the prisoners D'Erlach learned that Melendez had nearly recovered from the results of Ottigny's onslaught upon him, and that he was expecting the arrival of several vessels with men, supplies and horses, for his colony at St. Augustine, about the Christmas times.

The repulse given to the detachment led by Fernan Perez and his death, would doubtless deter any further attempt at finishing the destruction of the Huguenots until after that date. He reasoned also, that when the attack was made, it would be directly upon the post at Canaveral and probably take the form of a combined naval and land assault. The Chevalier prepared to join the main body immediately. At Ostinola's request he left Uhlrich and Ernest with ten arquebusiers and the wounded, seven in number, at the village to await further orders. These, with Ostinola's warriors, now imbued with confidence by the recent victory, could hold in check at least, any probable land expedition of the Spaniards until they could be reinforced. With the rest, D'Erlach embarked in the batteau, to which had been affixed a mast with a sail made from one of the captured tents, and with a strong northeast wind sped rapidly southward, having an Indian pilot on board.

Under ordinary circumstances, Ernest would have been very loth to part with his brother, but the circumstances were not ordinary. He was a favorite guest of the Cacique; his ambition was gratified by being placed in charge of the little company, his first military command; and—what was doubtless of more weight—a strong attachment had sprung up in his young heart for the flower of Toronita, the Princess Issena (so called by all). What was she? Only an Indian girl—a daughter of the sun and dew—a wild flower of the forest, a later Eve, and if the chronicles be not amiss, as true an one as she of Eden.

It is written: "There never was a fawn in all the forests more light and graceful in form and motion; never a bird that could sing a sweeter song; never a flower in any garden with a brighter face, and never beat in any bosom a truer, more faithful heart. So winsome in her natural ways was she, that it is no wonder our lord's brother" (this was written after the Chevalier had become the Seigneur D'Erlach,) "straightaway lost his heart to her, for indeed there was not one amongst us, but would have been her willing slave, had she but deigned to say that it would please her."

From the very first, the day when Ostinola gave the Huguenots a royal welcome, they had felt drawn to each other, yet neither knew why. With him, at first, it was simply surprise and admiration at her supple grace of motion, the brightness and beauty of face and form, the simple dignity of her carriage; but as the days went on, there were so many qualities of mind and nature constantly showing forth, that it ended in his complete surrender.

He was not learned in books; for in those days few save the clergy had much such knowledge. Books were far scarcer than swords and armor, and the master of the camp more common than the teacher.

But he could teach her the language of La France, and as he knew them all by heart the chaplain, when he departed, loaned him the little priceless book of hymns and poems with which he could instruct his willing pupil, in the rudiments of letters. He could also play the mandolin, and her deft fingers soon acquired the master's skill to sweep its strings.

Then there was a fairy world he could open up to her mind, in the stories of his native land that he loved to tell her, oftentimes as much by signs as words, as they floated on the river or sat beside the lightwood fire at eventide. And there were the marvels of land and ocean he had seen, and many other things to which she listened with rapt attention, as he described them.

While she in turn recited to him the traditions of the past, sang him the quaintest songs, and taught him the Indian names of flowers and birds, trees and plants, and all other objects in the little world around them. Indeed, there were so many things that she could teach him, that he often felt abashed in her presence, because of his ignorance.

Life was free to both. Whether by water or by land it mattered not whither they went. Passion as yet had not come to rock their souls to their centers as the earthquake does the earth.

It was the rosy dawn with them, when, cool, sweet purity of dews and morning zephyrs—the waking songs of birds—reigned supreme. That time in the poor lives of mortals their souls are nearest heaven; ere yet the scorching day heats come to wither the delicate flowers and fill the soul with fiery madness. That time, the poet souls of all races, kindreds and tongues, have sung of as the Eden day dawn, which was at the beginning and is forever, symbolized by all that is beautiful and lovely in earth and heaven.

CHAPTER XXVII

THE HUGUENOT EXPLORATIONS—A VOYAGE DOWN THE COAST TO CANAVERAL.

But little of the southern portion of these land-locked tide waters and their immediate shores had D'Erlach and his companions in the batteau seen before, for on their advance by land from the scene of the wrecking of the squadron to Matanzas, their march had been on the seaward side over the beach, which in his own words he described as "one of the finest in the world; being smooth, hard and broad enough for a large army to march over in ranked battalions, and though the sun might shine ever so brightly, moist with the tides and cooled by sea winds, seldom hot and uncomfortable." The absence of streams of fresh water, however, had made a resort to the wells at the Indian villages on the inner shores occasionally necessary, and on these visits only had they any views of this section of the country.

Now, however, the whole beautiful panorama was before them, each hour bringing a shifting of the scene, though all in perfect harmony.

Two leagues below Ostinola's town they came to an island, separated from the mainland by a salt marsh and a shallow winding creek behind which, and stretching a mile or more along the river shore, were the villages of Azalatowah, facing others on the peninsula side, each with shell mounds and little gardens very pleasant to the sight and containing quite a large population.

Indeed, there were more people here than at the town where the Cacique resided, and here was the original capital town of the tribe.

There was much rich land in the vicinity and more oyster reefs and bars in the river and a great abundance of fish. D'Erlach had examined the place during the resting time after the departure of the main body, with Ostinola, and had advised the latter to put up under Uhlrich's direction stockade defenses and in case of Spanish invasions to be prepared to retreat to it, as a more defensible position, both river and landward sides.

The breeze was fresh and fair and so they sailed on over the sunbright waters, only answering from time to time the friendly hails from either shore. Passing the southern point, jutting out into the main channel of the river which marked that boundary of the settlement, they sped on as if their boat had wings, over a broad bay, then passing another island, fairly white with herons, they entered a tortuous maze of mangrove islands and oyster reefs which extended to the inlet, in the neighborhood of which they were regaled at a village; where was a huge shell mound conspicuous from a distance; ruled over by a Cacique who was a friend and ally of Ostinola, and who, although doubtful at the first, whether his strange visitors might not be Spaniards, whom their traditions of former visits had taught them to be wary of, on hearing the report of their pilot received the whole party with pleasant welcome.

Still the many mangrove islets lined their way, as from this place they sailed on southward, threading them by such winding devious channels they were glad they had a pilot to direct them, until at evening they reached a high mound,* which seemed almost a mountain, from whose summit they could look far seaward, and southward over some wooded islands, beyond which stretched a great lagoon; whose waters sent back all the glowing colors of a gorgeous sunset in a thousand tints beyond the painter's art to imitate. Here also was an Indian settlement whose inhabitants received them gladly, as was their custom to the last, regarding the Frenchmen, for from their first contact, kindness had begotten friendship, broken by no hostile act, and not forgotten even in dire misfortune.

The general course of these waters was south with an easterly trend, and they were separated from the ocean only by a barrier which in some places was almost narrow enough for storm waves to leap over. All " abounded in fish and oysters, also large turtles, caught often by the natives sleeping on the surface of the water, or in traps and nets, they being excellent for food. Huge reptiles, called alligators, very much like the crocodiles of Egypt and India, but not so savage or feared by the inhabitants, were seen by us frequently; but as their skins are so tough as to turn spear point and bullet, and their flesh not to be prized for meat, no one disturbed them.

"Small sharks—which were not dangerous, however, to fishers wading in the waters or bathers, and immense sawfish, as they are called from their upper jaws projecting in the shape of a saw blade and being set with teeth, abounded; also porpoises or dolphins in great numbers. It was marvelous how many were the fish of all

---

*Note—Turtle Mound, on the Hillsboro south of New Smyrna. It has long been a land mark to sailors, along the coast.

kinds in these waters, the supply being kept up constantly from the sea; some of them being so grotesque in form and appearance that it seemed as if nature in this secluded region had much leisure to invent, as well as desire to multiply, strange creations.

"There was a great flat fish covered with a rough skin, having the mouth set with strong teeth more like those of a land animal than a fish, and having a long tail armed with barbed stingers or darts, whose wounds the Indians very much feared, being painful and dangerous to life. These darts were a palm breadth long and often used as arrow heads by the natives.

"We wondered very much at some large aquatic animals, for such they are, which grazed on the moss and weeds growing in many places on the bottoms of the deeper pools, especially where fresh water streams come in from the interior, in herds like cattle. They have no legs or feet, nor fins like fish, but are more like seals. Their flesh is esteemed by the Indians, but to us it was not very palatable. These water cows (or manatees) are not easily captured as they seldom come into shallow water or on shore, but when one is caught and killed a whole village will feast abundantly.

"Of wild fowl there is no end. Oftimes we would sail for hours through such immense flocks of ducks that they could scarcely swim or fly, they were so much in each others way; and when they did rise on the wing the noise they made was like distant thunder. Sometimes an arquebus shot amongst them would kill many, although fired at random. An expert bowman could with ease secure as many as he wished and very fat they were and good to eat."*

---

*Note—Even almost to the present year, Andreas La Roche's description of this section of the coast waterways, called the Halifax, Hillsboro and Mosquito Lagoons, is correct in every respect except as to the Indian villages, the only remains of which are the shell mounds.

CHAPTER XXVIII

THE CANAVERAL SHORE—THEY FLOAT THE DOLPHIN.

At the extreme southern end of the lagoon, where it was separated from a corresponding body of water by a narrow neck of land and also from the ocean by a similar strip, they reached on the next day the vicinity of the wrecks.

It was here one of the vessels, L'Etoile, came ashore and its battered hulk, stripped of masts, tackle and all portable articles, still remained a melancholy relic of the great storm. A short distance below was the hull of the Dolphin, the ship which Rotrou had commanded. It being staunch and new had so far resisted the power of the breakers, and by taking out of it all heavy articles, with anchors and strong cables seaward, they had tried to float it.

Near this, upon a sandy knoll, a rude stockade with huts had been erected and here were stored in hopes of final embarkation, everything of value rescued from the wrecks.

As the days went by in apparently futile endeavors, the hearts of the poor Huguenots had grown faint and sick. There was such a wild, strange wilderness of land and water around them, with the great ocean barring their way back to their native land. Morning and evening they gazed over its restless bosom hoping, yet dreading to see the white gleam of far off sails. The odds were so great that when they did see them they would not bear the flag of France or of friends. A little handful of people, whom their king loved not and in his treacherous heart had given up to the Spanish wolf, to do as he pleased with—the sails when they did show up were most likely to be those of their enemies, from whom they had but lately barely escaped with their lives.

It need not be said D'Erlach and his men were received with welcome, and the news of their victory over the Spaniards at Matanzas, for the time being, infused new life into them. Especially did it encourage Ottigny, LeCaille and Rotrou, the latter of whom, foreseeing possible failure in getting the Dolphin off the bar, had nearly completed a shallop, with which to navigate the inland waters or, perhaps, with good fortune, capture amongst the islands and keys to the southward, some Spanish craft. The Bahamas were not far distant, and they were much frequented by the Spaniards, who made a practice of visiting these islands and carrying off the natives in great numbers to Hispaniola and Cuba as slaves, until they were eventually depopulated. The shallop was soon launched successfully and the time came for the final attempt to float the Dolphin. It was an open roadstead exposed to the northeast gales, but the weather since the great storm had been mild and quiet.

The tides were now beginning to increase and there was a strain upon her moorings and a slight uneasy motion which showed that the ship was on the point of floating. To assist in this Rotrou had attached floats of timber and empty casks to its sides and one morning near the end of November, the trial was made to kedge it off.

Several anchors had been carried out, with the cables brought on board to the windlass. At the moment the tide lifted her free of the sand, a strain was put on them.

There was a moment of supreme suspense. A breaker coming against her made her tremble. "She moves!" shouted one. "Nay, she moves not!" exclaimed another. "Heave on the windlass, lads!" cried Rotrou. "Steady and all together.!"

When the cables were strained almost to parting, a great roller coming in lifted her off the bottom and the vessel moved forward. Seizing upon this hint every succeeding swell was utilized in like manner. But progress was slow and it was not until two days thereafter that deep enough water was reached to float the ship freely. It was then found there were so many leaks in the hull that it could not be kept afloat without pumping.

So some were kept busy at this, while others were employed in bending on the sails so that she could be taken to the inlet, beached and caulked.

What gladness and rejoicings there were, when once more sail was hoisted on the Dolphin! With what cheerful shouts they welcomed the rising to the masthead of their own flag! They wept and laughed by turns. Leaped and frolicked like children. There were some pieces of artillery which had been brought ashore and with them was fired the first salute that ever awakened the echoes of this coast.

Long afterwards the Indians told of the day of thunder, when there were no clouds.

The drums beat. Luigo's bugle played every strain of joy known to him and there was no cessation of rejoicing amongst those temporarily left behind to care for the stores, when Rotrou filled away on the seaward tack to make an offing for the inlet.

Fortune was once more smiling on them, or at least seemed relenting.

"Praise God! The good ship Dolphin is afloat once more!" said Le Roche. "Surely she should be called our Good Hope," said another, and so on they spoke merrily and hopefully to each other. Although there were some, who said but little; in whose eyes the tears stood, not for sorrow, but for gladness too deep to voice in words.

They seemed to see, far beyond the waters, the sunlight falling on their native hills in a sheen of glory; lighting up the vales and vineyards; the orchards and fields of corn; the haven of Rochelle, crowded with shipping; its ramparts holding in stout embrace their homes and home folks—nay, they seemed to hear mingling with the moaning of the surf breaking at their feet, the very market cries; gay songs of revelers, or hymns of praise and thanksgiving; not loud, because coming so far, yet clear enough for their souls to hear and be thrilled through and through.

Amongst those left behind to guard and transport the stores, there was a young man who sat upon the bank with his head upon his hand, silent for a while, gazing after the ship. "What ails thee, mon ami?" queried a comrade, placing his hand upon his shoulder.

"Thou knowest, LeBarron, I ran away and joined Monsieur Ribault's ship, because I thought life at home was a torment, but I am heartsick to hear Dame Marjorie scold again. I would rather hear her make the saucepans fairly rattle with her tongue, than listen to the angels' singing; for look you, then I would know that I was at home once more!"

"Ah lad!" LeBarron answered, looking at the swelling of the Dolphin's sails as she bowed to the billows, "There be others that would like to drink a tankard of red Burgundy in thy mother's inn, and with God's help they may." And with Hope's song in their hearts they gazed seaward lost in dreams of home.

CHAPTER XXIX

THE SPANIARDS SEEK TO DESTROY THE HUGUENOTS—THE BATTLE OF AZALA.

A few hours after the departure of the Dolphin, LeBarron came to D'Erlach, who was superintending the transportation of stores to the shallop and reported that off the cape could be seen the gleam of far-off sails.

And so it proved, for as the sun set low in the west its rays beat full and fair against the white canvas of four vessels steering northward, coming close enough to land for the French to distinguish their hulls.

These, by their fashion and size, were judged rightly to be the squadron Melendez expected, but as the vessels kept on their course no alarm was created. Rotrou meantime had gained his harbor before the Spanish vessels came into sight and was hidden from them. He sought and found a suitable place for finishing the repairing of the Dolphin, in a deep creek out of sight from the inlet, behind dense thickets of mangrove trees, where for a fortnight the work went on undisturbed.

Melendez at St. Augustine, upon the arrival of the ships containing soldiers, colonists, horses and supplies although having so much to engage his attention in the more securely establishing of his colony as to prevent him from leading it, could now send a detachment to retaliate upon the Huguenots the destruction of the outpost at Matanzas, doubting not that it would be an easy matter to over-master the remnant of Ribault's forces.

To the several Spanish cavaliers, too proud to work or be deeply interested in the building of forts, houses or settlements, the lack of opportunity to display their military spirit was very irksome. So when the Adelantado's intention of attacking the Frenchmen was made known there was eager strife amongst them as to who should lead.

It had been learned that a small detachment of Huguenots was with Ostinola but that the larger party was at Cape Canaveral, or supposed to be, for those on board the squadron, coasting along near to land had noted the wrecks, also the little stockade and had seen men busy about them.

So, while a detachment of two hundred soldiers was placed under the command of Diego de Maya for the land attack, Martin D'Ochoa was given two large caravels with as many more on board, to assault the Canaveral post.

As for D'Ochoa, his expedition was a fruitless and not dangerous one, for on his arrival he found the locality deserted by the French. He, however, burned their huts and stockade. Nor could he find any trace of their whereabouts, for upon his appearance the Indians of the neighborhood fled to inaccessible haunts on the inner islands.

But Maya's expedition had different results. It landed secretly at night from boats on the south side of the Matanzas Inlet and once more the dawn of day gleamed on helm and corselet, and the beach side showed a long marching column, for besides the soldiers there were slave porters and camp followers after the fashion of the times, making quite an army.

There were friars also, carrying the crucifix, for this was a Christian invasion of a land whose inhabitants were pagans and heretics.

At evening they came to a little village at the head of the river, whose inhabitants, not able to resist, fled in dismay; several being shot as they ran through the forest or towards the shore as if they had been but wild beasts. Whatever was left behind, of use to them, the soldiers looted.

On the next day when they came to the village opposite Ostinola's town, this, too, they found deserted and although across the river could be seen signs of people moving, having no boats wherewith to cross, it was determined to halt and send out scouts to find the enemy. Nor was it long before these reported that at a place two leagues below, both on the mainland and peninsula shores, were many Indians gathered to dispute their further progress.

Maya divided his forces into two parties, the larger one to march southward by the beach, the other carrying only their arms, by a little central valley and seeing that reinforcements were constantly going by water, he hastened forward.

THE BATTLE OF AZALA.

The main body pressed rapidly onward until suddenly a stinging hail of arrows fell on them from the high bank along the seashore. Shouting their war cry of 'Santiago! For Leon and Castile!" the Spaniards rushed up the steep, sandy banks and rapidly drove the Indians back towards a high central ridge. Here they were suddenly halted by a volley of bullets from young D'Erlach's squad of arqubusiers.

It came so unexpectedly upon the Spaniards, there was a lull for a moment, but soon firing on the north told of the other detachment having reached the scene of action. Then rose a clamor of Indian war whoops, Spanish and French war cries mingled with the reports of firearms and other sounds of battle, such as these wilds had never known before.

Several assaults were led by DeMaya in person, but were beaten back bravely.

Ostinola and his warriors were fighting for their homes, their liberties and lives. The Huguenots knew no mercy was to be expected from such foes. But the Spaniards were well armed and so armored that the chances of loss in battle from the weapons of the Indians were small. Their steel caps and breastplates were impervious to the arrow shafts, but several in the close encounter were beaten to death with clubs, and sometimes a well-aimed arrow or spear point found a defenseless spot.

Then the thickets were so dense and filled with stubborn, agile foes, that headway was difficult as well as dangerous.

Ernest D'Erlach and Uhlrich with their little handful of arquebusiers and a number of Ostinola's men with halberds, but not well skilled in using them, formed the very core of the defense, and perceiving this, Maya sent his best men against them and here the battle waged the hardest. At last an Arragonese soldier skilled as a marksman, got a shot at the young lad that brought him to the ground, but as he was in the very act of uttering a shout of triumph, Itahoma, with unerring aim sped a shaft from his strong bow, which drove right through his eye into the brain. At this moment the flanking party of Spaniards drove back the Indians before them and Maya ordered his men to charge.

This forced the Indians and the little company of Huguenots back toward the river shore, fighting every foot of the way. Along the riverside there was a long straggling village with gardens. A portion of this was seized by the Spaniards, but another portion, somewhat apart from the rest, which had rude palisades about it and contained a large shell mound, was stoutly defended by the Indians and Huguenots, until sundown, when the battle ceased.

The grief and consternation of the Huguenots was indescribable when they found Ernest was missing. None but Itahoma had witnessed his fall and he could only tell how a Spaniard had fired at him, and that young D'Erlach fell immediately, but that the brush was so thick he could not see him any more—"Neither," he added grimly, "could the soldier who shot him."

The night was dark, but both Itahoma and Uhlrich stole through the woods to the scene of the main battle and searched for Ernest, but found him not. There was anxiety also amongst them over the disappearance of Issena, who, with her favorite companion, Nonotta, although they had come to the village in the morning, was not to be found anywhere.

CHAPTER XXX.

THE LAD'S DESPERATE PLIGHT—ISSENA'S HEROISM— D'ERLACH TO THE RESCUE.

On the eve of this first day of the battle of Azala, the rays of the descending sun, poured through all the wide horizon rich floods of radiant color, glorifying land and sea and river, into a dream of heaven.

They illumined the curling wreaths of battle smoke with rainbow irridescence, and piercing through the ranks of forest trees, fell on bruised leaves of plants and blades of grass, all dabbled and stained with the red tide that is the life of mortal men; and lying in the midst of them, upon the stiffening forms of those who never more would strive in desperate battle, and on the wounded writhing in pain, clamoring for water. 'Twas Nature's lesson, that despite its covering of pomp and glory, war is never aught but hell.

Already treading on the heels of the last charge, which drove the battle toward the river shore, were the Spanish camp followers searching the hillsides and the valley with their daggers ever ready to give short shriving to the Indians left behind, disabled by their wounds.

"Why spare them? They are but pagan dogs! Send them to their father, Satan!" This was their only logic, emphasized by steel.

Still echoed the sounds of the contest raging fiercely around the village; the sharp reports of arquebuses; the clash of swords and halberds; war whoops and battle cries; with anon a bugle blast or war conch's wild dissonance, mingling in a barbarous discord, answered from the sunfilled heights of air by the screams of soaring eagles.

At this time, and near the spot where the Huguenots had stood to meet the foes onslaught, the bushes were parted and two young girls stepped forth into the open.

One said: "Near this very place I saw him last. I marked it well, for I could see, against the gray trunk of this gnarled oak, the gleaming of the egret plume I dyed for him myself and fastened but yesterday on his morion —for so, he said, the ladies of his land were wont to do by their chosen knights—and truly he was mine. And yet I see no trace of him, though only a few short moments have passed since then.

"As the Spaniards poured over the crest of yonder hill, there came a volley from all the arquebuses that filled the air with thunder and smoke, so that none could hear or see. Then came the rush of the charge, and as his comrades were beaten back I saw he was not with them."

They were Issena and her faithful friend Nonotta, venturing on the battlefield in search of the younger D'Erlach, and as they looked hither and thither, hoping, yet dreading, to find what they sought, Issena called out: "Ernest! My Ernest, where art thou?"

There came no answer, save the mournful burden on the air and then she uttered low: "My heart will break if I find him not. And yet—when I do find him—it may still break. Oh thou, his God and mine, I pray Thee let me find him! He is too young and fair and brave to die! If he be dead, how can my soul, to whom the way is strange, find his in Heaven?"

From various points of the valley and hillsides, thickly set with tall spruce pines, bent toward the west by sea winds, with underneath tangles of low shrubs, broken and bent still lower by the trampling of many feet, came groans and cries to which she turned a listening ear; eager to catch a tone she would know full well, but could not hear amongst them all.

The summit of the seaward ridge was not far and from it came the sound of voices. They turned their faces towards it and saw a group of black-robed men, gazing downward. The friars had found the Arragonese arquebusier still alive, with Itahoma's arrow shaft fast in his head and he, so far as concerned this life, past all praying for or surgery. Then arose upon the air the old Latin service for the dying.

Listening for a moment and seeing that from this source, not soon at least, would come interference with them, the two continued their seeking, until Nonotta pulled back a sweet bay branch hiding a little hollow and exclaimed: "See, Issena! Here lies the young chief! He looks as if he slept, but I do fear he is—"

"Nay! Nay! Say it not! I cannot, will not have it so!" And springing forward Issena flung herself beside the outstretched form, lying face upturned, with set lips and staring eyes that saw not.

One hand still tightly gripped the sword he had drawn to meet the Spanish charge; the other lay upon the ground as if to stay himself in falling; and taking this in hers, she uttered in words mingled with sobs and tear-drops falling like rain; "Oh, my love! If thou canst not speak aloud, whisper! Be it but one word—if ever so faint and low—I will hear it in my heart. Or, if not even that is in your power, do but move your lips to frame a word or make your eyelids quiver, that I may know thou art not gone from me forever."

She ceased and gazed fixedly on the pale, cold face before her; heedless of the near sounds or farther echoes of the cruel war still raging near them. To her it mattered naught.

The world had slipped away from her and was as if it had never been. Over her young soul the waves of desolation were sweeping, and she was drowning in them, nor cared to make a single effort. If he were dead, what was it all to her?

Then she placed an arm under his head and raised it, gently speaking in his ear: "I call thee, mon ami! Canst thou not hear me? If thou art going to that far bright land thou hast told me of so often, tarry a little while upon the way that I may join thee!"

She kissed him. There was the faintest breathing of a sigh. The eyelids closed. She put her ear to his breast as if to listen to a heart beat.

Of a sudden, a ray of hope lighted up her countenance just as the summer lightning does a Gulf Stream cloud.

"Oh, Nono, my friend! He lives! His heart still beats! Quick! Grasp my hands underneath him—so! They must not find him here to finish slaying him."

Tenderly they raised him in their strong young arms and bore him swiftly down the glade, not toward the village, for the enemy was between them, and the fighting not yet over.

Ere the shadows of the twilight came upon them, they reached a little pool of water in a deep hollow, far enough away for present safety, where underneath the oaks and palmettos, in a spot bare of aught but soft leaves and grass, they laid their burden down.

From the clenched fingers they took the sword; unloosed the steel cap, in which Nonotta brought water; while Issena, heedless of the blood stains, save as they moved to more tender care and pity, unfastened the lad's bullet-torn doublet and found so jagged and great a wound, made by the ploughing bullet, it took all the spirit from her, making her mourn and tremble.

And yet, they did, between them, so manage to bind up the wound with such knowledge of healing leaves gathered near, as staunched the farther flow of blood; helped by the cold insensibility so near akin to death, it was hard to tell the difference.

Twilight deepened into night. To this hollow deep amid the forest and thicket-covered ridges, came the booming of the surf as if miles away. The branches overhead shut out the stars. There was no wind, only a ghostly mist came floating in, which they could feel in its chill and dampness, but neither see nor hear. But naught came to harm them.

And by his side, through the long dark hours, in the little bower of palmetto leaves they had built, Issena sat, while the soul of Ernest struggled back to sensibility; listened to his every sigh and inspiration, with his hand in hers; gave him water; cooled his forehead or soothed him with words he himself had taught her; glad despite the pitch black gloom, that their service of love and pity showed some reward.

At last the weary vigil was broken, just before the dawn of day, by the strains of a bugle coming sweet and clear from the river.

It was Luigo blowing. The Chevalier was coming to the rescue. An answering strain—it was LeBearnois telling where the beleaguered Huguenots were.

Then farther still, arose the clamor of the Spanish trumpets and drums calling to-arms.

CHAPTER XXXI.

THE HUGUENOTS GAIN ANOTHER VICTORY.

There was a thick mist on the river, enough to hide the shore from a little distance out upon the water even when the day dawn came to tinge its fleecy folds with roseate hues; but guided by LeBearnois' bugle, the Chevalier, with a fleet of canoes, filled with warriors from the lower river villages gathered on his way, and fifty of his own men, steered straight for the position held by Uhlrich and Ostinola, which De Maya had prepared to carry by storm in the morning. But now, not knowing the full strength of the reinforcements, and judging rightly that they were headed by D'Erlach himself, De Maya was convinced that he must add discretion to valor and rapidly made preparations for either fight or flight as need be. However, he would first assault and try their strength so sent a hundred arquebusiers to assail the stockade.

This detachment from the cover of the nearest dwellings, suddenly began heavy and rapid firing, sending a hot storm of bullets upon the Huguenots and Indians, promptly answered in like manner. In the midst of which fusilade D'Erlach landed.

A few words from Ostinola and Uhlrich informed him of the condition of affairs, also that Ernest was missing; that Uhlrich and Itahoma had themselves searched the battlefield and found no trace of him, nor did they believe he was in the hands of the Spaniards.

Meantime the latter were pushing the contest so vigorously, it was necessary to repel them, before aught else could be done.

Perceiving that the houses, although slightly built, concealed their foes from sight, arrows wrapped with inflammable materials set on fire, were shot into their roofs of thatch, which speedily caught in flames, driving the Spaniards back.

Under cover of the smoke, flanking parties of Indians were sent out which were speedily met by De Maya's falling back toward the beach.

The trails through the timber and thickets by which they retreated were narrow, and with some of his best men De Maya held back all assaults, until from behind the high sea ramparts he could employ his whole force in the battle.

But every moment, his enemies thickened and drawing closer to his lines, poured in upon them such galling, stinging showers of arrows, that at the last discouraged by the utter impossibility of overcoming the allied forces, he began the retreat towards Matanzas, leaving several of his best men slain.

De Maya had surely stirred up a nest of hornets and all along the coast line he had to fight his way northward until sunset put an end to the contest in the vicinity of Le Camp Reconte Felice, where he camped that night, and from whence on the next day he retreated to St. Augustine.

It is said that this expedition thoroughly convinced the Spanish captain that there was neither glory or profit to be derived from waring with these coast tribes, and that soon afterwards he left Melendez' service and joined the conquistadores of South America.

Meantime, how fared it with Issena and her charge. When the two heard the bugles blowing, for they were not so far from the river shore that the sounds could not reach them distinctly, hope filled their hearts. Help surely was near at hand. But when at daylight came the echoes of renewed battle, they listened with anxiety.

The sound of firing aroused Ernest somewhat from his insensibility. His voice was faint and he could only mutter brokenly: "I hear the arquebuses—the battle goes on—and I—what means this—my side pains me so!" Then looking up into the face of the form bent over him with the daylight falling fair upon her features, he added: "Is it thou, Issena? Take my hand—I scarce can lift it." And so, apparently content, he relapsed into silence, so motionless, so marble-white his face, it seemed certain that death had set its seal upon him.

Soon there drifted in upon them, filtering through the forest growth, streams of pungent smoke. What if the woods were on fire and the hungry flames should come leaping in upon them? They would scarcely dare to move him for fear of starting his wounds afresh. Nor would they know where to fly for safety. They knew not where their friends were, or their enemies. What could they do but await the issue of the battle, meantime clearing a circle around them of the dead leaves and underbrush, so as to keep back the fire should it come.

An hour longer they listened until the clamor of the battle grew more distant by which they knew the enemy was retreating. Then came the trampling of men through the thickets following their own little path down the glade.

The two girls sprang to their feet, and in a moment

there rang a shout of discovery as the foremost of the searchers, an Indian, saw them.

Following on his heels came D'Erlach himself, with others. His eyes saw in a moment the little bower; the lad's sword leaning against a tree trunk; the stained doublet and morion. His tongue uttered but this: "My brother, is he here?" "See, my lord!" answered Issena, removing a broad palm leaf so that he could look upon Ernest. "Nay," she exclaimed, as D'Erlach started, thinking he was dead. "He is alive, but so grievously hurt I fear much for him. All night long his soul seemed on the point of flight and sometimes I thought it was so, and then my heart was very heavy."

Then she told him all the story, and true hearted soldier as he was, the Chevalier kissed her hand and so thanked her for her loving loyalty, that to her dying day she forgot not his words.

Andreas Le Roche was somewhat skilled in surgery, both by study and experience, and after a brief examination, said the lad stood a chance of recovery with care and nursing, and that what had been done was well done, but that extreme caution must be used in moving him to better quarters. A courier arriving at this moment said the Spaniards were making a stout defence at the seaside, so D'Erlach rapidly made what arrangements were necessary to transport them all across the river to the main village, and hastening back to the contest, animated anew by finding Ernest still alive, soon made such disposition of his forces as started the Spaniards on their retreat up the beach, thus driving back the last invasion for many years of Ostinola's territory.

Towards evening, Ottigny and Uhlrich came back to

Azala with two prisoners, whom they had captured in the attack upon De Maya's retreating forces. They had recognized them as members of the assassin band that had slain Ribault, nor did the men deny it, but rather gloried in the deed. Earlier in the day one of the friars also had been taken. So a council, after the fashion of a military court was called, composed of Ostinola, his chief men and the Huguenot officers, who tried and condemned the assassins to be put to death. They were accordingly bound to a tree and shot to death with arrows, the friar being permitted to give them his services and then the latter was turned loose to rejoin his defeated countrymen.

And so ended in victory for the Huguenots their last battle with the Spaniards on this coast.

THE DOLPHIN WINS HER PORT—THE JUNE DAY AT ROCHELLE.

How shall the rest of the story be told? Just as the old Chronicle tells it.

It was the evening of a June day, A. D. 1566, in fair Rochelle, the brave old city by the waters.

Amongst the shipping in its harbor, moored fast to the wharf, was the battered, worn hulk of the Dolphin, and close by as frayed and wave worn by billows and tempest, a Spanish galleon from which floated beside the flag of France, the D'Erlach banner.

Only the morn before, these two vessels, close to each other, sailed by the Isle de Re, with colors flying, sails full spread, trumpets blowing; answering the culverins of the fortress at the harbor's mouth, with their own "bastards and mynions" and brass guns of Spanish make, in noisy salute; making fast to the landing amidst the shouts of the burghers and sailors of the Huguenot city, gathered there to give them welcome.

Albeit there was sadness soon, overcoming their rejoicing, when it was seen how few they were who returned from that far, strange land, whither had sailed from this very port, Ribault's gallant fleet. And there were many, both men and women, the latter chiefly, who crowded on board the vessels to ask how it had fared with this one, that one, or the other; too often going slowly homeward with bent heads or weeping sorely.

Amongst them came a comely matron, with eye alert and springy step and white kerchief, stiff as starch could make it. In a moment she had sought and found a young man, the comrade of LeBarron, and placing a hand upon his shoulder said: "Is it thou, Ambroise Elide? I could scold thee good, thou runaway, but my heart is too glad!" and then she fell to weeping.

It was Dame Marjorie, who had found her son, and he flung his arms around her, saying: "Scold, mother mine, an thy heart will let thee, for it will be sweeter music than I have heard for many a weary day."

One trod along the gangway plank leading to the galleon's deck, for whom the throng made respectful way. He had on a dark gown with band of white about his neck and wore a black skull cap, the whole costume, severe and plain, as became the chief preacher of Rochelle, Master Keppel, the guardian of Ribault's daughter, the Lady Jeanne.

He came as one expecting sad news, for from his window overlooking the harbor he had seen the vessels coming in and had marked the absence of Ribault's own ships.

To him D'Erlach told the whole story of Ribault's fate. Showed the script and signet ring the general had given him in charge; and set apart that evening to deliver the same into the daughter's own hands. Then brought to him his brother Ernest, still pale and thin as scarce recovered from his wound, with the Princess Issena and her faithful Nonotta, and asked that the Lady Jeanne might, as soon as her sorrow would permit, take charge of the maids. This and more, was on the first day of arrival.

The evening of the second day, LeBearnois, Antoine Uhlrich, the Florentine Luigo, LeRoche and LeBarron, were bidden by Ambroise to his mother's inn, where Master Keppel was to join them, as Dame Marjorie wishẹd much to hear all they could tell "for that addle-pated son of mine can give neither head nor tail of the story."

So they went at his bidding; passing up the well-known narrow streets, paved with cobble stones and lined with quaint old buildings; by the burghers' council hall, the church and market, and entered the inn door just as dusk fell and the cressets were lighted; showing up the long low dining room with its red-tiled floor, and tables heaped with good cheer; not forgetting great flagons of wine, with the Dame's best silver tankards to drink it from, polished like mirrors. And when they had eaten much and drank but little, she and Master Keppel, who had joined them, pressed them to tell the story of their mishaps and wanderings, while her maids and neighbors gathered near to listen.

Andreas at first was spokesman, but before it was all told, each joined in to tell a part and as they spoke their hearers sighed, wept or shuddered, but seldom smiled.

The story was finished by Le Bearnois, who told how, after the battle of Azala, "where the friars ran so fast they tripped upon their gowns," the Huguenots finished the repairing of the Dolphin; gathered with the help of Ostinola and his men such stores of provisions as the country afforded and they needed; filled their water casks; received many presents of dressed skins, Indian fabrics and curiosities; and how lastly, when they were ready to depart, Ernest declared he would not part from Issena or she from him, nor Nonotta from her, and so it was finally settled between the Cacique and the Chevalier, that the two should go with them to France. Also how, upon the last day, came the Cacique's wife, Cowena, bringing an earthen pot of pearls and many other rare things that would make the two damsels quite a fortune.

"Fair and sunny was the morning, when the tide turning seaward, the signal gun was fired. Then our flag rose proudly to the masthead; our sails filled to the breeze and with our prow turning the wavelets into foam, accompanied to the very breakers on the bar by Ostinola and his flotilla of canoes, we laid our course for France."

"But where fell you in with the Spanish galleon?" asked Master Keppel.

"Why, that was a stroke of good Providence in our favor. There is off the coast of Florida a great group of islands called the Bahamas, sometimes the Isles of Bohemia. Soon after we left port there came up a heavy north gale, which despite all we could do, drove us southward. We had none on board who knew aught of the seas around these islands, but by good fortune we ran under the lee of one called Abaco, and there we found and surprised the galleon. After mastering the crew we set them ashore to shift for themselves as best they could, they being better acquainted with the country and we so overcrowded on the Dolphin as to be uncomfortable. We found also considerable treasure on board and provision, whereat we rejoiced greatly, for that we should not suffer from empty stomachs or come home empty-handed."

The tale was ended as the moon arose, flooding towers and ramparts, the city's clustering dwellings and the harbor with its mellow light; and they, being joined by others from the ships, beneath the clustering vines of the arbored garden of the Inn, hanging full with unripened grapes, the air fragrant with the breath of roses, sang and danced for hours, glad to their souls to be home once more in La Belle France.

APPENDIX

It will be seen by the historical facts given in this Story of the Huguenots that they were the first martyrs to civil and religious liberty on the North American Continent; arriving as they did nearly half a century before the landing of the Puritans at Plymouth. Their trials, sufferings, and the tragic deaths of many of them, while not resulting in establishing a permanent settlement, sanctified the land to liberty, although more than two hundred years elapsed before a final victory was achieved for human freedom and the greatest republic on earth was established.

Another fact is shown by history: The Huguenots driven to America by intolerable oppression, from first to last, have filled our chronicles with gallant and patriotic deeds and the names of their descendants stand high on our rolls of honor, in every walk of life.

INDEX

----, Bartholomew 56-57 88
  Marjorie 176 194-195
ATINAS, Martin 29
BALBOA, 14
BROOKS, A M 91
CHARLES, King Of France
  35
CHEMIN, Jean Ressegui De
  57
COLIGNY, 36 59 94 109
  Adm 10 13 19 33 90
COLUMBUS, 147
CORTEZ, 14
D'ALEMBERT, 87 111 120
  Robert 81
D'ERLACH, 17 21 25-26 77-
  81 83-88 91-93 100 103-
  104 108-114 120-123
  128-129 133-137 139-141
  147 150 152-153 156-161
  165 168-169 174 178 181
  184 189 192-194
  Alphonse 77 Chevalier
  18 85 Ernest 88 94 111
  121-122 128 165 181-182
  184 187 189 192 195-196
  Monsieur 83 88-89
  Seigneur 166
D'OCHOA, 90 107 179
  Martin 90 179 Senor 90
D'OTTIGNY, 107 Chevalier
  80 Louis 105
DEAVILA, Pedro Melendez
  35 43 69 91
DEGOURGUES, Chevalier
  100
DEHAIS, Jean 28
DELAGRANGE, 64 80
  Sieur 70 79 86 95
DELASMERAS, Solis 98
DELAVEGA, Garcelaso 98
  Garcilasco 148 Garcilaso
  147
DELAVIGNE, 53 Capt 88
DELEON, 13-14
DEMAYA, 181 189-190 193
  Diego 50
DEMORGUES, Jacques
  Lemoyne 150
DEOCHOA, Martin 124
DESOTO, 13-14 Ferdinand
  9
DEVALDEZ, Diego Flores
  99
DEVALOIS, Margarite 132
DEVARVAEZ, Pamphilo 9
DIAZ, 159 Diego 158
ELIDE, Ambroise 194
FERDINAND, King 147
FRANCE, King Of 33

GOURGUES, De 62
GRAJALES, 99 Priest 98
HAIS, Jean De 57
HARNEY, 27
HAWKINS, 30 32 Adm 29
   57 John 31
HERRERA, 147
HULRICH, 92
INDIAN, Cowena 135 140
   196 Issena 166 182 184-
   185 187 191-192 195-196
   Itahoma 134 152 156
   182 185 189 Nono 186
   Nonotta 182 184-185
   187 195-196 Olata 24
   Olata Utina 21-25
   Ostinola 122 129 132-
   133 135 137-140 151-153
   156-157 159-160 162-166
   168-169 179-181 189
   192-193 195-196
ISABELLA, Queen 147
JACKSON, 27
JEAN, Francis 49-50 55
KEPPEL, Master 89 194-
   196
LACAILLE, 87 93 111 120
   Francis 81
LAGRANGE, 97-98
LAROCHE, 172
LASCASAS, 147-148
LAUDONNIERE, 13 15-17
   19-24 28-34 40 44-46 49
   53-58 60 79 121 147
   Rene 10

LEBARRON, 176-178 194-
   195
LEBEARNOIS, 103-105 107
   115-116 122 131-132 137
   151 157 188-189 195
   Perrault 91
LECAILLE, 174
LEGENRE, 17
LEROCHE, 164 176 195
   Andreas 139 156 192
LORRAINER, 78
LUIGO, 112 115-116 151
   175 188 195
MARTYR, Peter 147-148
MAYA, 179-181 Deigo De
   179
MELENDEZ, 10 38 41 43
   45 47-56 58 60-63 66 68-
   70 74-83 86 88-90 92 94-
   95 103-107 109 111 119-
   120 124 160-161 165 178
   190 Pedro 36 Pedro De
   61
MENENDEZ, 97-100 108
MIDDLETON, George C 96
MORGUES, Jacques Le
   Moyne De 57
OCHOA, 75 124-125 Martin
   De 50 53
OTTIGNY, 17 25 78 81 91
   103-106 115-117 119-120
   122-125 139 165 174 192
   Capt 93
PATINO, Andres Lopez 53

PEREZ, 158-159 Fernan 52 157-158
PERRAULT, 104 115 Francis 103
PHILIP, Ii King Of Spain 35 King Of Spain 69 90
PIZARRO, 14
PONCEDELEON, 5 143 Juan 9
PREVATT, Bartholomew 55
RECALDO, Francis 50 53
RENE, Monsieur 55
RIBAULT, 13-14 29-30 32-33 36 38 40-42 44 46-47 49 57 63-66 73-82 84-85 87-88 90-100 103 106 109 111 119-121 136 158 176 178 193-194

RIBAULT (cont.) Jean 10 34 91 Jeanne 89 194-195 M 69 76
ROTROU, 85 87-88 91 93 111-112 114 139 156 174-176 178 Pierre 81 84 120
SALVANDI, 125-126 Father 49 60 124 Friar 126
TAYLOR, 27
UHLRICH, 86-88 111 122 136 158 165 169 181-182 189 192 Antoine 85 195
VASSEUR, Capt 17
VILLAREAL, Gonzalo De 59
WARDWELL, Capt 131
WOLFINGER, Leslie 13

Made in the USA
Charleston, SC
29 July 2010